Training Too Much?

*A Sceptical Look at the Economics of
Skill Provision in the UK*

J. R. SHACKLETON

*Principal Lecturer in Economics,
Polytechnic of Central London*

IEA

Published by
INSTITUTE OF ECONOMIC AFFAIRS
1992

First published in June 1992

by

THE INSTITUTE OF ECONOMIC AFFAIRS

2 Lord North Street, Westminster,
London SW1P 3LB

© THE INSTITUTE OF ECONOMIC AFFAIRS 1992

Hobart Paper 118

The Institute gratefully acknowledges financial support for its publications programme and other work from a generous benefaction by the late Alec and Beryl Warren.

Printed in Great Britain by

GORON PRO-PRINT CO LTD

6 Marlborough Road, Churchill Industrial Estate, Lancing, W. Sussex

Text set in Berthold Baskerville

CONTENTS

LIST OF TABLES AND FIGURES:

[5]

FOREWORD

International economic comparisons were once in fashion. Typically, the supposed poor performance of the British economy was attributed to differences (as demonstrated by statistics of some aspect of the economy or society) between Britain and her principal competitors. Our 'problem' was that we had insufficient investment (either in general or in some chosen area), there were too many unions, unions in general had too much influence on government, marginal tax rates were too high, management was poor, there was too much expenditure on welfare, defence spending was excessive, or we had no incomes policy. The possibilities were endless. Since, whatever the chosen indicator, there would always be differences between Britain and at least one competitor, differences in economic performance could always be attributed to there being 'too much' or 'too little' of something in this country. The inevitable next step was to argue that the government should intervene to put matters right.

The search for such explanations is no longer so intense, nor is the analysis generally so naïve. In the light of experience, belief in omniscient and altruistic governments has faded. In any case, there seems less to explain now that Britain's economic performance has improved relative to that of other countries. Nevertheless, as Mr Shackleton explains in Hobart Paper 118, in the field of training old habits persist. There is still a consensus— stemming primarily from comparisons with competitor countries, especially Germany—that British workers are underskilled and that a considerable increase in government investment in training is required if the economic performance of competitors is to be matched. That consensus exists even though it is difficult to find any positive correlation between the resources a country devotes to training and its rate of economic growth.

Is there an economic case for a further expansion of training provision at state expense, inevitably accompanied by regulations about training, to add to the already very considerable expansion of the 1980s? Mr Shackleton is sceptical. He points out that not only are labour and other factors of production substitutes one for another, but that skilled and unskilled labour are also substitutes: there is no 'right' way of producing a given output which applies to all countries. Nor is there a 'right' way of producing a given degree of skill—it is not clear that formally qualified and certificated workers are invariably more skilled than those with less formal training acquired on the job. Rigid rules, which lay down the amounts which companies should spend on training, are also of doubtful value when different industries have very different skill requirements.

The increase in government expenditure on training of recent years may, according to the author, have had little to do with the economic case for such provision. Much of it may have related to the perceived political urge to be seen to be 'doing something' about unemployment. Whatever the reasons, a 'jungle of job creation and training schemes' has been created with a number of undesirable features, including monopolies of initial training and the validation of vocational qualifications. There may indeed now be an over-emphasis on vocational qualifications which is potentially dangerous to the extent that it assumes the demand for future skills can be anticipated.

State expenditure on training shows every sign of having increased without any thought being given to the economic principles which should govern such expenditure. The argument that markets will, unaided, provide insufficient training has been too readily accepted. In fact, there is no reason to believe that specific training will be under-provided by markets since employers will expect to appropriate the benefits in terms of a better trained work-force. There is more reason for concern that general training will be under-provided since employers will find it more difficult to capture the benefits. They may fear that they will train workers only to have them poached although, as Mr Shackleton explains, the evidence does not suggest that such fears seriously inhibit training and in practice there appears to be considerable private provision of general training.

If, nevertheless, one accepts that some degree of market failure is possible, what is the appropriate policy response? Since the British government has operated anything but a 'hands-off' policy in recent years—central government spending on 'training and enterprise' rose from less than £1 billion to nearly £3 billion (in 1990-91 prices) between 1978-79 and 1990-91—the government is already spending heavily to correct supposed market failures in training. It is not legitimate to argue that, because in principle market failure may exist, still more needs to be spent centrally. Indeed, it is possible that the government is already spending too much on training or is directing expenditure into the wrong channels. Unless there is clear evidence of the extent of market failure—which there evidently is not—we cannot judge whether the government is doing too much or too little to assist training provision.

Furthermore, whenever government action is suggested as a remedy for market failure, the extent to which government will itself fail ought to be considered. According to Mr Shackleton, the scope for such failure is considerable. Not only do governments have a powerful incentive to be seen to be doing something in labour markets at times of high unemployment, there are many interest groups which now prosper from the availability of large state funds for training and which therefore press for such funds to be increased.

Employers can benefit if the state pays for training which they would otherwise have provided themselves. Some companies may be only too happy with regulations which force their competitors to train more than they would wish, thus inhibiting competition and providing a barrier to entry. Unions and professional bodies also favour training schemes which impose qualifications and limit the supply of labour into particular occupations. Employees may see training as a 'perk' if there is an element of on-the-job leisure at conferences and courses in pleasant locations. And there is now a large training industry, depending significantly on government for its support, which stands to gain from increased taxpayer contributions to its activities. Mr Shackleton also sees signs that the new TECs are becoming pressure groups calling for more state spending on training '. . . in a way which goes far beyond what civil servants would have been permitted to do when they were running training schemes' (below, page 79).

The author concludes that, important activities though training and education are, one should hesitate to accept the arguments from vested interests in the field that they should take increasing amounts of taxpayers' money, '. . . imposing obligations on employers or individuals to meet their skills requirements in a particular way, or to force education into a vocational straitjacket' (page 81). We should, instead, be sceptical of those who claim to know 'which skills will benefit the economy better than the individuals and firms involved' (page 81).

Analysis of markets—how they work and, in some cases, how they may fail to work—is the main concern of the Institute of Economic Affairs. It has, over the years, published many dissenting views from authors sceptical of the received wisdom in their own fields of expertise. Mr Shackleton's paper is in that tradition. Although the views expressed are his and not those of the Institute (which has no corporate view), its Trustees, its Directors or its Advisers, his *Hobart Paper* is published by the Institute as a significant contribution to discussions about the economics of training provision.

May 1992　　　　　　　　　　　　　　COLIN ROBINSON
Editorial Director, Institute of Economic Affairs;
University of Surrey

THE AUTHOR

J. R. SHACKLETON is Principal Lecturer in Economics at the Polytechnic of Central London and a member of PCL's Education, Training and the Labour Market research group. He was educated at Calday Grange Grammar School, King's College, Cambridge, and the School of Oriental and African Studies, University of London. He previously taught at Queen Mary College, London, and has worked as an economic adviser at the Department of Social Security. He has written or edited books and monographs, including *Twelve Contemporary Economists* (editor, with Gareth Locksley, Macmillan, 1981); *Wages and Unemployment* (Employment Research Centre, University of Buckingham, 1987); *Economics* (with L. W. Ross, Longman, 3rd edition, 1991); *Sunday, Sunday: The Issues in Sunday Trading* (with Terry Burke, Adam Smith Institute, 1989); and *New Thinking in Economics* (editor, Edward Elgar, 1990). He has also written widely in journals, reviews and the press. He is a member of the Council of the Royal Economic Society.

ACKNOWLEDGEMENTS

Useful comments and criticism on a draft came from Professor E. G. West, Sir Douglas Hague, Walter Allan and Geoffrey Killick. More general ideas about training have been discussed with Barbara Roweth, Andre Clark, John Walls and Siobhan Walsh. The section on public choice owes a lot to Len Ross.

J.R.S.

I. INTRODUCTION

There is a remarkable consensus in the UK that we have a seriously underskilled work-force, and that enhanced training provision is the key to the country's economic regeneration.

Academics such as historian Corelli Barnett[1] and economic commentators such as Sig Prais of the National Institute of Economic and Social Research (NIESR)[2] see our failure to produce a work-force as well-qualified as that of Japan or Germany as the chief reason for Britain's long relative decline.

This analysis has found attentive ears across the political spectrum. Conservative administrations under Mrs Thatcher and Mr Major have been very active in this area of policy. The 1991 White Paper[3] was only one of a bewildering list of policy initiatives. Throughout the 1980s central government spending on a variety of training schemes rose steeply while other areas of public expenditure were held down. Despite recent attempts to cut back on training expenditure, it is still costing us well over £2 billion a year of public money.[4] Much of the educational system is being reshaped to meet the imperatives of the labour market, and a new government-sponsored scheme of certification of vocational qualifications is having an increasing impact. Private employers are being exhorted as never before to provide or help fund training, play a key rôle in running the Training and Enterprise Councils (TECs), and contribute to the governance of schools and colleges.

The Labour Party, too, 'believes in a training revolution for Britain'.[5] Together with the Liberal Democrats (who advocate compulsory training for two days a week for all employees aged

[1] C. Barnett, *The Audit of War*, London: Macmillan, 1986.

[2] Frequent references to the major research programme on training at the NIESR are given in this paper.

[3] *Education and Training for the 21st century*, Cm. 1536, London: HMSO, May 1991.

[4] This is central government spending on training and enterprise schemes only. The most recently published figure for all government spending in this area put it at £7 billion for 1986-87. In the same financial year training costs incurred by individuals and employers were estimated at £8 billion and £18 billion respectively. (*Source: Training Statistics*, London: HMSO, 1990.)

[5] *Modern Manufacturing Strength*, London: The Labour Party, February 1991, p. 11.

[13]

16-19), Labour vies with the Conservatives to devote increasing public and private resources to training. They are joined by the Trades Union Congress, the Confederation of British Industry and the Institute of Directors,[1] whilst the Director-General of the National Economic Development Office, Dr Walter Eltis, has argued that 'improvements in our training are central to our industrial future'.[2] Virtually every economic journalist of note has taken a similar line, and a growing army of 'trainers', educators and consultants preach the gospel to anyone who will listen.

To the sceptical economist, however, such unanimity raises a shadow of a doubt. Can it really be the case that increased formal training provision is the panacea that UK policy-makers have sought for so long? Or is it just another patent medicine hyped out of all proportion by self-interested promoters? Should we really be seeking to spend large sums of public money (or persuading firms to spend money they would not otherwise have done) on a huge expansion of training opportunities?

If we believe it to be necessary to intervene in this way, we must believe that training is a particularly drastic case of 'market failure'—where the free market, left to itself, systematically under-provides training. Why should this be the case in the UK to an apparently greater extent than elsewhere? What, anyway, is the precise rôle which training plays in the economic process and in the generation of economic growth? And, if we concede that there may be some underprovision of training, are current policies likely to improve matters—or could they perhaps worsen the situation?

This *Hobart Paper* cannot answer all these questions, but it can at least probe a little behind the rhetoric. The purpose is not to denigrate the effort and time put into training by individuals and employers, but rather to attempt a cool and disinterested view of this major economic phenomenon.

---

[1] See, respectively, Ron Todd, 'Skills: Towards 2000', in John Stevens and Robert MacKay (eds.), *Training and Competitiveness*, London: National Economic Development Office and Kogan Page, 1991; 'Achieving the Skills Revolution', Memorandum by the Confederation of British Industry, London: CBI, 21 December 1990; *Performance and Potential: Education and Training for a Market Economy*, London: Institute of Directors, 1991.

[2] See his Preface to Stevens and MacKay, *op. cit.*

II. TRAINING AND THE ECONOMY

The British economy has been in decline relative to other developed countries for a long time (by some accounts since the second half of the last century, and certainly since the Second World War). Of this there can be little doubt, although the extent of the decline can be exaggerated and the British often seem disposed to take the gloomiest possible view of their circumstances.

For many years, then, the search has been on for an explanation of decline—preferably one carrying the potential for policy recommendations which will reverse it. Currently the focus is on inadequate training as the cause of our problems, and massively increased investment in training as the panacea. A cacophony of abuse is likely to greet anyone who questions this new Conventional Wisdom.

One of Many 'Explanations' of Economic Decline

Yet it is as well to remind ourselves that other explanations have been just as confidently propounded in the past. A partial listing would include: inadequate investment in new technology, high marginal tax rates, too much state involvement in industry (or too little, or the wrong kind), a concentration on finance rather than manufacturing, combative or subversive trade unions, the lack of an incomes policy, the burden of the welfare state, excessive defence spending ... plus grander ideas such as Our Failure to Have a Modernising Revolution.[1]

Many of the proposed remedies have been attempted. In some cases they have actually been implemented more or less as specified (lower marginal tax rates, trade union reform)—but the problems remain. Great amounts of government expenditure have frequently been involved, often completely wasted,[2] and the private sector has been repeatedly urged to alter what it sees as profit-maximising behaviour in order to hold down prices, to

[1] In this view successful 'modern' economies have to make a decisive break with their past, scrapping pre-capitalist institutions and creating a political and social climate conducive to money-making.

[2] John Burton, *Picking Losers ...?*, Hobart Paper No. 104, London: IEA, 1983.

[15]

buy British, to take on extra labour, to stand up to unions, and so on. Is reform and expansion of training the Holy Grail we have sought so long, or will it be yet another disappointment?

Aggregate Evidence

It has to be said that the evidence in favour of the view that training is crucial to economic performance at the aggregate level is less than overwhelming. Clearly the human factor in economic activity is important, but where exactly training comes into the picture is much less clear.

In the 1960s, economists devoted a great deal of time to trying to explain differences in rates of growth between countries by using newly available macro-economic data. Doyen of these specialists was Edward Denison, whose best-known book, *Why Growth Rates Differ*, was published in 1967.[1] Denison's method was, briefly, to apply an *aggregate production function** (a mathematical expression linking inputs of the services of factors of production to total output or national income) to an economy. He would attempt statistically to explain changes in output over time by reference to changes in quantities of inputs. Such exercises, carried out by many economists, typically left an 'unexplained residual' which could not be accounted for by changes in the total quantities of labour, land, and capital (as conventionally measured) available. This was thought to be the result of improvement in the quality of the labour force over time. To support this hypothesis, it was shown that a substantial proportion of this residual could be accounted for by measures of educational achievement in the labour force. So the 'residual' was correlated with measures of educational achievement. Denison-style studies[2] showed, however, that there were diminishing returns to formal schooling, with most of the benefits coming from the achievement of universal primary and secondary education.

*Words and phrases set in italics and followed by an asterisk are defined/explained in the 'Glossary', below pp. 82-84.

[1] E. F. Denison, *Why Growth Rates Differ: Post-war Experience in Nine Western Countries*, Washington DC: The Brookings Institution, 1967. Interestingly, in view of current obsessions, Denison found that education accounted for 13 per cent of national income growth in the UK in the 1950s and early 1960s, but for only 2 per cent of Germany's growth, suggesting perhaps that education was not a crucial element in relative performance.

[2] Reviewed in George Psacharapoulos, *Returns to Education: An International Comparison*, Amsterdam: Elsevier, 1973.

This methodology can be (and has been) criticised.[1] But the point is, even accepting for the moment that it is plausible, that it does not enable us to infer anything about training. Clearly training embraces some formal education, but much else besides. Arguably it interacts with formal education, rather than being simply additive to it.[2]

The Comparative Dimension

In any case, there are very few indicators of training available on a similar basis from country to country. The only officially published measure is the proportion of 16 to 18-year-olds in full- or part-time education or training,[3] which is available for 13 OECD countries, including the UK, for 1986. My own calculations show that this indicator displayed a *negative* (though statistically insignificant) correlation with growth performance of the relevant countries over the decade 1979-89. Although it is possible that more sophisticated econometric work could uncover a robust positive relationship between quantitative indicators of a country's training inputs and macro-economic performance, I remain sceptical.

Many experts would argue that it is not quantity but quality of training that counts. I shall explore this argument further below (in Section V, pp. 51-75). The question was, however, examined fairly closely by the Central Policy Review Staff just over a decade ago. They concluded that

> 'it is difficult, if not impossible, to *prove* that particular features of a country's training and education systems are associated with high or low levels of productivity'.[4]

Despite the concentration of the brightest and best brains of the Think Tank, they 'were unable to identify any single issue where a major government initiative would radically improve

[1] See E. Cohn and T. G. Geske, *The Economics of Education*, New York and London: Pergamon Press, 3rd edition, 1990, Chapter 6. Cohn and Geske also provide a review of more recent empirical work on this subject.

[2] It is well established, for example, that those with higher educational qualifications are likely to receive more on-the-job training from employers than other workers. This makes it difficult to separate the returns to training from the returns to education.

[3] Published in *Training Statistics*, London: HMSO, 1990, and summarised in my Table 11 (below, p. 45).

[4] *Education, Training and Industrial Performance*, Report by the Central Policy Review Staff, London: HMSO, 1980.

the responsiveness of the system' to the world of work.[1] As we shall see, neither the Government, nor the Opposition, nor a thousand and one interest groups have been prepared to accept such a conclusion. First, however, some economics is necessary.

[1] *Ibid.*, p. 3.

III. THE ECONOMICS OF TRAINING

It is not easy or straightforward to define 'training'. In a descriptive sense, training encompasses a wide variety of ways in which skills are enhanced.[1] To an economist, skilled labour is seen as an economic resource with some characteristics which it shares with other economic resources—and which are sometimes inadequately grasped by non-economists. For example:

(i) *It is an important input into many productive processes, but like other inputs, there are substitutes for it.*

Economists understand that, in the production of most goods, there are many different ways of producing similar outputs, using different combinations of resources. The appropriate method to choose is that which is the cheapest (i.e., most economical), given the relative prices of productive services. Hence the increasing emphasis placed by development economists on 'appropriate technology': it makes no sense for countries or regions where capital equipment is expensive and labour cheap to use the same production methods as countries or regions where capital is cheap and labour expensive. Similarly, different combinations of skilled labour, unskilled labour and machinery are feasible ways of producing a given output. To take one example: in some parts of California where Hispanic labour is widely employed, tills in fast-food restaurants are designed with pictures of the appropriate items on the keys, thus reducing the necessity for staff to be literate in English. To take a more pertinent example, studies seem to suggest that British and German firms use a different 'mix' of skills to produce engineering output. British firms use graduates and higher technicians in rôles which in Germany are more likely to be taken by the more numerous workers possessing intermediate skills. Hart and Shipman suggest that

---

[1] The government-sponsored *Training in Britain* study, for instance, concentrates on 'formal, structured and guided' means of acquiring work-related skills, but excludes general supervision, motivational meetings and basic induction; the Employment Department's publication, *Training Statistics*, however, adopts a broader definition which covers 'any intentional intervention to help the individual or organisation become competent, or more competent, at work'.

'British firms can often sustain the output of sophisticated products, in spite of a largely unqualified work-force, by optimising the allocation of qualified labour between tasks and by relying on uncertified skills acquired through experience'.[1]

In neither of these cases am I suggesting that such practices are ideal, merely possible. As David Metcalf has put it:

'[T]he possibility that less skilled labour is substitutable for more skilled labour, and *vice versa*, needs careful investigation prior to any evaluation of vocational training.'[2]

(ii) *Similar reasoning suggests that a given level of skill can also be 'produced' in different ways.*

Common sense tells us that particular skills can be obtained through a variety of means: formal 'off-the-job' education or training (part-time or full-time), formal 'on-the-job' employer-provided training, distance learning, formal time-serving apprenticeship, informal work experience, and so on. The skills acquired may be certificated or uncertificated.[3] Current thinking in Britain compares the relative dearth of formally qualified individuals with the position in some other countries and asserts that far more formal training, appropriately certified, is required; but the grounds for this assertion are rarely spelt out. By contrast, for most goods or services, consumers neither know nor care by what process they were created.

(iii) *Although skills can be substituted to some degree, it is clear that some industries are always going to be very 'skill-intensive' while others have much less need of skills.*

Yet despite this fact, employers who do not provide much training are routinely castigated for this omission. Thus Labour

---

1 See P. E. Hart and A. Shipman, 'Financing Training in Britain', *National Institute Economic Review*, May 1991, p. 77. See also H. Steedman, G. Mason and K. Wagner, 'Intermediate Skills in the Workplace: Deployment, Standards and Supply in Britain, France and West Germany', pp. 60-76 in the same issue.

2 D. Metcalf, *The Economics of Vocational Training: Past Evidence and Future Considerations*, World Bank Staff Working Paper, No. 713, Washington DC, 1985, p. 74. Metcalf reports evidence that *elasticities of substitution** (measures of the ease with which productive resources can be substituted in the production process) between different types of skill are in practice positive and relatively high in many fields.

3 Many workers who lack formal skills may have picked up considerable expertise through 'sitting next to Nelly' and keeping their eyes open. This is increasingly recognised by those concerned with training: the National Council for Vocational Qualifications, with its approach to testing for competences, and the movement for the Accreditation of Prior Experiential Learning in higher education provide testimony to this. It will be suggested in Section V, however, that there are dangers in such accreditation.

TABLE 1

EMPLOYERS' VOCATIONAL TRAINING COSTS
AS A PERCENTAGE OF TOTAL LABOUR COSTS:
GREAT BRITAIN, 1984

Industry	With apprentice wages included	Without apprentice wages included
Food, drink and tobacco	0·6	0·3
Chemicals	0·9	0·4
Metal manufacture	1·0	0·4
Mechanical engineering	1·7	0·4
Instrument engineering	1·5	0·4
Electrical engineering	1·7	0·5
Shipbuilding	3·1	0·7
Vehicles	1·9	0·4
Metal goods	1·2	0·2
Textiles	0·7	0·1
Leather goods	0·8	0·1
Clothing	1·2	0·1
Bricks, etc.	1·1	0·1
Timber, furniture	1·3	0·2
Paper, printing, etc.	0·8	0·2
Other manufacturing	0·9	0·3
Construction	2·6	0·4
Distribution	0·8	0·2
Banking, insurance, finance	0·7	0·6

Source: Dept. of Employment, *Labour Costs Survey*, 1986.

Party policy is to require that at least 0·5 per cent of a company's payroll be devoted to training, whatever it produces.[1] This would be highly arbitrary. As Table 1 demonstrates, statistics of the costs of training are sensitive to the *definition* of training costs included.[2] There are considerable variations in measured

[1] See *The Independent*, 5 February 1991.

[2] One recent authoritative study admits that 'Information on training expenditure is very imperfect. . . . Reported expenditure varies enormously, and both understates true costs . . . and the activities which can be construed as training'. (*Training in Britain . . .*, Vol. 3: *Employers' Perspectives on Human Resources*, London: HMSO, 1989, p. 19.)

training costs from industry to industry, but there is no obvious pattern of 'successful' industries devoting more to training than 'unsuccessful' ones. In any case, a rule requiring that a minimum proportion of expenditure should be spent on training lacks any clear rationale in economic theory. Given that firms' labour forces differ enormously in average skill levels, pay rates, proportions of full- and part-time workers, training cost structures, average age, and so on, such a rule could serve only as a (costly) gesture of support for the principle of expanded training opportunities.

Human Capital

Bearing these considerations in mind, I now consider the incentives to provide training. If training is a means of enhancing the productivity of human resources, it is useful to think of it as a form of investment in 'human capital'. Like all investments, it entails costs today in anticipation of future benefits. Such costs include the resources directly used in training (the salaries of trainers, buildings and equipment used in the training process, and so on) plus 'opportunity costs'—that is, benefits forgone by engaging in training. For trainees these will include the difference between pay received in training and what could be obtained by the trainee in an unskilled job. For employers these may include the difference in productivity between a trainee worker and a fully-productive worker paid at the same rate, and the return forgone on resources tied up in training.

The benefits or return on training investments by employers will be the value of the higher productivity which the trained worker can offer the employer; for employees, the benefits primarily appear in higher rates of pay on completion of training.[1] In order for it to be worthwhile for training to be provided, the value of the benefits (suitably discounted to reflect the fact that they occur in the future) must be at least equal to the costs.

Individuals and the Decision to Train

This way of thinking about training is best illustrated by a (highly stylised) diagram such as that of Figure 1. Think about a 16-year-old school-leaver who has two alternatives facing him or her. One is to take an unskilled job which initially pays a wage of £X

---

[1] Though job security may increase and there may also be 'psychic' benefits—increased status or enhanced pleasure in work.

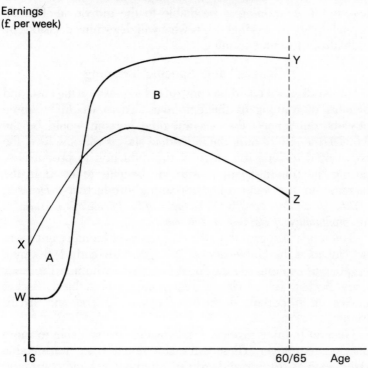

Figure 1:
Costs and Benefits of Training to the Individual:
The Human Capital Approach

per week. The curve XZ traces out the individual's '*age-earnings profile*'* until retirement if he or she stays in this job; for unskilled work, earnings tend to rise with age until the late thirties or early forties and then decline.

The alternative is to undertake a course of vocational training. Initially the trainee receives a lower pay rate, £W per week, to reflect the fact that his or her immediate productivity is reduced whilst being trained. As training is completed, pay rises. Increased skills are assumed to mean higher productivity, for which employers will pay more. At some point the earnings of the trained worker overtake those of the unskilled, as depicted by the curve WY. It is often assumed that age-earnings profiles for skilled workers will flatten out rather than decline with age, as productivity is less dependent on physical effort and stamina than is the case for the unskilled.

In Figure 1, Area A indicates the costs incurred by the trainee:

[23]

in this example, purely *opportunity costs**. Area B represents the gross return on his or her training. If what accountants call the *discounted present value** of B is larger than that of A, the investment in training is profitable to the individual. Human capital theory asserts that this is what will determine decisions by individuals to enter training.[1]

'General' and 'Specific' Training

A similar diagram could be constructed to illustrate the costs and benefits of training to the employer. There would be some obvious differences: the relevant time horizon would be the expected length of time the individual stayed with the firm, the cost would include the value of the reduction in productivity during the training period, with the benefits reflected in the increase in the value of post-training productivity. *However, whether or not these benefits can be captured by the employer is crucial to the profitability of training in this model.*

The modern approach to the economics of human capital was developed at the University of Chicago in the early 1960s by a number of economists, the most famous of whom is Professor Gary Becker. In his classic treatment[2] of the subject, Becker makes an important distinction between *general* and *specific* training.

General training produces skills which are valuable to more than one employer. These will include quite basic 'transferable skills' such as reading and writing, interpersonal and communication skills—but also higher skills of a more specialised nature. A qualified electrician possesses general skills; so does an economist. They can expect to find a wide range of employers who will be willing to pay them more than unskilled workers.

By contrast, Becker distinguishes specific training as 'training that has no effect on the productivity of trainees that would be useful in other firms'.[3] Examples he provides include training as an astronaut (valuable to NASA, but not elsewhere), and resources spent familiarising new employees with a firm. We

[1] The human capital approach to training has roots in the work of Adam Smith in the late 18th century. It was understood in part by Alfred Marshall a hundred years later, though he did not try to 'operationalise' it. Marshall, incidentally, was an early enthusiast for the German system of training: see his *Principles of Economics*, 8th edition, London: Macmillan, 1920, p. 175.

[2] Gary S. Becker, *Human Capital: a Theoretical and Empirical Analysis*, New York: Columbia University Press, 1st edition, 1964, 2nd edition, 1975.

[3] *Ibid.*, p. 26.

could add examples such as training for a particular company's computing system or stock-control system, or as a tour guide to a particular stately home or theme park.

The distinction is not an easy one to maintain, as much training involves elements of the two types. Even something like astronaut training produces, as a side-effect, skills which are valuable elsewhere (as a test pilot, for instance, or, more prosaically, in public relations: few ex-astronauts have difficulty getting such work). Holding down any sort of a job in one firm may also be a useful indicator to another employer that you possess some valuable attributes—at least, when compared to another job applicant with no such experience.

Who Funds Training?

Clearly, though, some forms of training are much more 'general' while others are much more 'specific'. This is economically relevant because of the implications which the distinction has for the funding of training.

Becker points out that employers have an incentive to provide 'pure' specific training. Investments in such training enhance the productivity of workers to the particular firm, but not to other employers. As the workers' skills have no enhanced value outside the firm, the employer does not have to pay higher wages to prevent them being poached away by other employers. The *value marginal productivity** of specifically skilled labour exceeds the wage-rate paid. Thus the whole of the benefits of investment in specific training can be captured by the firm, making such investment potentially profitable.[1]

By contrast, the benefits of investments in general training are assumed to be much more difficult for employers to capture. Individuals receiving general training have their marginal productivity enhanced in a wide variety of potential employments. In a competitive market they may be enticed elsewhere by employers who are willing to pay for the increased value of their services; alternatively, the employer providing training will

[1] Again, this is a simplification. Workers leave firms for various reasons, not all to do with the pay and other characteristics of jobs. If there is a high turnover amongst the work-force, specific training is less profitable. In order to reduce turnover, employers may often offer higher rates of pay to keep specifically trained workers, even though these workers' specific skills have no 'outside' value. Thus the returns from specific training are shared. In turn, they may be able to share the costs with workers. Incremental pay scales may be devised which involve a career ladder within a firm. This may be attractive to workers even if initial pay is thus artificially lowered.

have to pay skilled workers more to retain them. In either case, it is argued that it will be unprofitable for employers to provide such training because of their inability to capture the returns on their investment.

There are exceptions to this inability, of course. Where employers can prevent trainees leaving immediately on completion of their training, it is possible for them to recoup the costs of their investment. As indentured labour is now illegal, however, the armed forces are one of the few employers able to do this. In the UK, as elsewhere, the Army, Navy and Air Force provide a large quantity of general training. Since members of the armed forces sign up for long periods, their employers gain the benefits of general skills for equally lengthy periods.[1] Similarly, if there are information imperfections in the labour market, or barriers to mobility between firms, generally-trained workers may be retained even though they are paid less than the value of their marginal productivity.

Apprenticeship

Otherwise, the human capital approach predicts, employers will be unwilling to pay for general training, and in a free market the costs of the investment will fall on employees (or their parents). Such general training may be obtained in schools, universities, polytechnics or colleges. But we should remind ourselves that it may also be provided by employers, though effectively paid for by employees.

The clearest form of such an arrangement is the apprenticeship (a system of providing general training which goes back many hundreds of years). Here the apprentice effectively pays for his or her training by taking very low wages during the training period. The employer pays less than the value of the employee's marginal productivity during training, in effect using the difference to pay for the training cost. On completion of training, skilled workers are paid the full market value of their

---

[1] Discussion of this issue can be put in the context of the economics of property rights. Different 'rules of the game' mean that incentives are structured differently. If employers providing training were able to claim a 'transfer fee' from employers who enticed workers away, presumably the provision of general training would be more attractive to employers. However, the experience of professional sports suggests that the restrictions such a system places on employees are unacceptable in modern conditions. And no one country can unilaterally impose such a system of property rights in a world where labour is increasingly mobile across frontiers. Nevertheless, the White Paper, *People, Jobs and Opportunity* (Cm. 1810, London: HMSO, February 1992), proposed precisely this solution. The suggestion is to use industrial tribunals to enforce 'training contracts'.

TABLE 2

APPRENTICES IN MANUFACTURING INDUSTRIES, 1964-89

	Numbers (thousands)	Percentage of employees
May 1964	240·4	3·0
May 1974	139·6	2·0
May 1979	155·0	2·2
March 1984	82·0	1·5
March 1989	53·6	1·0

Source: Training Statistics 1990, op. cit.

skills. Although we tend to associate apprenticeship systems with manual skills, rather similar principles are involved in the system of pupillage for barristers, and the low rates of pay and poor conditions of junior hospital doctors: trainee barristers and doctors in effect pay for their general training in this way.

Formal apprenticeships have been in long-term decline in this country, though there is also a cyclical pattern. In the 25 years from 1964 to 1989, the numbers in manufacturing, for example, fell from nearly a quarter of a million to just over 50,000 (Table 2).

The reasons for this decline include structural changes which have reduced the size of those sectors of the economy traditionally taking large numbers of trainees; high levels of unemployment; increases in training costs which have made this method of finance less feasible; a substitution of certificated, college-acquired skills for traditional time-serving; a rise in the relative pay of young unskilled workers which has dimmed the attractions of reduced pay during apprenticeship; and the growth of government-sponsored training schemes such as YTS (now Youth Training).

Market Failure?

Becker's analysis is useful in pinpointing potential sources of 'market failure'. This is defined as a situation where the free competitive market may produce a less-than-optimal outcome: in this case, may provide less training than is judged to be desirable on some wider grounds.

[27]

In Becker's framework, there would seem no obvious grounds for market failure to occur with *specific* training, assuming that firms are reasonably well-informed about their production processes and the pre-existing abilities and skills of their workers. If investment in specific skills is seen as likely to raise productivity by a sufficient amount (suitably discounted) to cover costs, firms should be able to recover their investment; an adequate amount of specific training is therefore likely to be provided.[1]

The problem, then, seems to lie with general training. Although the free market is evidently able to provide a large amount of general training, the possibility of market failure arises for a number of reasons.

One is that the most basic general skills of literacy and numeracy need to be inculcated at an early age, most effectively in schools. Economists have long recognised that there is some sort of a case for compulsory schooling on the grounds that parents may not always be the best judge of their children's wellbeing.[2] Up to what age this argument applies, however, is a moot point. Arguably many children have clear ideas and preferences about their prospects which need to be given appropriate weight well before the school-leaving age of 16.[3] It seems difficult to find any reason for enforcing compulsory full-time education beyond that age, as some interested parties[4] have recently suggested (although one may accept that there might be advantages in larger numbers *choosing* to stay on at school).

[1] There may be a problem if labour turnover is excessively high because of distortions elsewhere in the economy—say, because social security rules allow people to leave jobs voluntarily after short periods and claim benefits. However, it seems unlikely that this is a major problem in the UK today. In any case, labour turnover here is not particularly high by international standards.

[2] However, the strength of this case (accepted in part by J. S. Mill, amongst others) has been challenged. It is claimed that compulsory education may have come about as a result of pressure from producer interests such as teachers and educational bureaucrats rather than the intrinsic merits of the case: see E. G. West, *Education and the State*, London: Institute of Economic Affairs, 1965, 2nd edition, 1971; and *Education and the Industrial Revolution*, Batsford, London, 1975, Chapter 16.

[3] It has escaped widespread comment that the effective school-leaving age has recently been raised by requiring all students reaching age 16 between 1 September and 31 January to stay on at school until the end of the following Summer term, rather than allowing them to leave at Easter or May as previously. (See *Education and Training for the 21st Century*, Cm. 1536, London: HMSO, May 1991, Vol. 1, p. 46.)

[4] For example, the 'G10' group of TECs (see below, Section V, p. 65).

Financing Training

Another frequently asserted source of market failure[1] lies in the difficulties facing individuals in financing general training. In principle, such training can be financed privately in three ways:

(i) through reduced wages during training;

(ii) from savings by individuals and their families, or income transfers within families;

(iii) by borrowing.

There are problems with each of these methods. Take the first: in many occupations, training costs may be so high that they cannot conceivably be financed by reduced pay alone; in any case employers may not, for a variety of reasons, offer such training contracts. So far as I know, no employer offers basic training as a professional economist: you have to get a degree first.

Family circumstances differ from individual to individual, and are not perfectly correlated with ability to benefit from training. Although many families could undoubtedly afford to pay for their children's education and training, many certainly could not.

In a perfectly functioning capital market, it might be assumed that workers could borrow sufficient funds to finance training, just as firms in such a market could borrow to finance physical investment which promised a rate of return equal to the *opportunity cost** of funds. However, in the real world it is not usually possible to borrow from the private sector on the necessary scale to finance lengthy training without collateral, simply on the prospect of a higher income in the future.

The upshot of this is the view that the market, left to itself, will under-provide general training. Yet it must be emphasised that this is not a foregone conclusion. Businesses, trusts and charities frequently sponsor general training and education even though there is no direct pay-off to them from so doing. It is also worth reminding ourselves that much general training involves 'learning-on-the-job' where skills are produced as a 'joint product' with the firm's output. If the firm is to produce at all, it must therefore train, explicitly or implicitly.

---

[1] There are still others which have been discussed, including imperfect information and *risk-averse** attitudes by employees which lead them to under-invest in training.

Market Failure and Government Failure

These considerations notwithstanding, the policy conclusion usually drawn is that the state should intervene in some way to encourage a higher level of training than the free market would offer. It may do so by providing free or subsidised training from public agencies, schools and colleges, or by paying private sector firms to provide training (either directly or through some form of voucher or training credit), or by placing obligations on firms to provide training, or by providing grants or loans to individuals. Funds may come from general taxation, or levies on firms, or repayments of loans previously made to individuals.[1]

It should be noted as a general principle, that interventions of this sort have to be carefully designed if they are not to prove costly and wasteful. For example, levy-financed schemes are typically costly to administer and fail to cover all those who are supposed to pay the levy. Recovery of government loans from some groups of workers may be extremely difficult. Subsidies to the employment of some groups of trainees (such as the young) may create unemployment elsewhere (older workers). In this area, as in many others, there is the potential for considerable 'government failure' to set alongside 'market failure'.

Rates of Return

The human capital model sketched earlier led to a methodology for calculating rates of return on educational and training courses. Treating a course of study or training as an investment, economists have calculated the rate of return on the resources explicitly or implicitly (for example, the opportunity costs of earnings forgone during training) invested.

Such calculations can be done for both the *private rate of return** and the *social rate of return**, an important distinction when the state subsidises education and training. It is assumed that the private rate of return motivates decisions by individuals and firms, while the social rate of return may be a guide to appropriate public policy. Most frequent attention has been paid to returns on higher education, where the focus is on the individual rather than the firm and the returns are easier to calculate, though in principle the methodology can be applied to

---

1 For a useful discussion, see P. E. Hart and A. Shipman, 'Financing Training in Britain', *National Institute Economic Review*, May 1991.

TABLE 3

PERSONAL AND SOCIAL RATES OF RETURN TO TAKING A FIRST DEGREE IN THE UK, 1981-85

	Personal Rates %	Social Rates %
Social Sciences	32·5	12·0
Engineering	34·0	7·5
Sciences	23·5	6·0
Arts	10·0	0·5
All subjects	27·5	8·0

Source: Dept. of Education and Science, *Top-up Loans for Students*, Cm. 520, London: HMSO, 1988.

any type of training or education. In this case the costs of education to the individual are reduced by grants or loans from the state (though note that the private returns to the investment are also reduced by the tax paid on higher earnings after qualification), and so the private and social rates of return differ. Table 3 shows some examples of the results of calculations of this sort.

These figures tell some interesting stories. They demonstrate the extent of the subsidy provided to students in higher education, and formed an important plank in the case for introducing student loans.[1] But they also show us some of the difficulties involved in drawing other policy conclusions.

On a personal level, taking a degree is clearly worthwhile. But notice that there are considerable variations in rates of return between different subjects. This is a finding which is common to other studies, and seems likely to be an 'equilibrium' rather than a 'disequilibrium' phenomenon. This compares oddly with the predictions of a simple theory of resource allocation, where investment funds move between competing projects leading to equalisation of marginal rates of return on different investments.

Social science (which includes business studies, almost certainly

[1] Social and private rate of return calculations for the United States typically show lower private and higher social rates of return, reflecting the fact that students usually finance a larger proportion of their own educational costs in America. For a review of the US evidence, see Cohn and Geske, *op. cit.*, pp. 105-14.

considerably boosting the average return for this group) and engineering degrees have a high private rate of return, but sciences offer significantly lower returns to individuals. This is a result which has frequently been found, and may partly explain the relatively small numbers of young people opting to study the sciences. Arts subjects, however, have a very much lower private rate of return. We might expect that very few students indeed would wish to study the arts, but this is not the case. It is traditional—and plausible—to argue that arts degrees offer 'non-pecuniary' benefits to compensate for their poor career prospects. But the necessity for such *'ad hoc'* explanations tends to reduce the predictive power of the human capital model.[1]

The figures for social rates of return, again displaying a pattern familiar from other studies, raise intriguing questions. The negligible social rate of return on arts degrees is perhaps not surprising,[2] but the other relativities are: in particular, the differential between the social rate of return on engineering/sciences and social sciences. Does this mean that resources should be shifted into social science/business studies training rather than engineering?

Perhaps that is exactly what it means. Some commentators, however, have pointed out that what the rates of return figures reflect is the financial return in terms of higher pay on completion of higher education. It is commonly assumed in economics that pay reflects the value of workers' marginal productivity. But this is true only under competitive conditions. If markets are distorted in some way so that pay does not directly reflect the individual's productive contribution, social rate of return calculations are misleading.

And there are some reasons to suggest that this may be the case. According to one source:

'the industries to which most engineering and science graduates are recruited have a lower typical salary progression than areas such as banking and finance'.[3]

---

[1] A point made by Mark Blaug in his article, 'Human Capital Theory: a slightly jaundiced survey', *Journal of Economic Literature*, Vol. 14, No. 3, 1976, pp. 827-55.

[2] Though the policy conclusion is not clear-cut if there are strong *external benefits**, uncaptured by these data, from the existence of a substantial arts community. For example, tourism may be stimulated. Such an argument, however, tends to open the floodgates to special pleading.

[3] National Economic Development Office, *Industry and Education: Memorandum by the Director General*, London: NEDO, March 1991, p. 14.

Moreover, the pay of chartered engineers ranks markedly below that of groups like business economists and lawyers in industry.[1] Yet, at the same time, engineering consistently tops the list of occupations for which employers report skill shortages,[2] suggesting that the labour market for this type of skill does not work in the manner that the simpler economics textbooks describe. It is therefore possible that labour in engineering is paid less than the value of its marginal product, though why this should be so in this specialisation rather than others remains obscure to market economists.[3]

Some sceptics argue that employers' statements about shortages should be treated with a pinch of salt. Milton Friedman[4] observed long ago that business people's opinions about their behaviour were about as valid as octogenarians' explanations for their own longevity. More recently, Oliver and Turton have expressed doubts about the nature of the skill 'shortages' which employers often report, arguing that they are often bemoaning the lack of particular attitudinal or behavioural traits which training alone cannot impart.[5]

'Screening' and 'Credentialism'

There is a line of thought which expresses more general doubts about the use to which the human capital model has been put as a guide to policy. This is the view that general training and education—at least, as measured by formal qualifications—adds little to individuals' marginal productivity even though it adds to their earning power.

This apparent paradox is resolved by the argument that training and education provide employers with a way of 'screening' for more highly motivated and proficient individuals,

---

[1] *Ibid.*, p. 16.

[2] *Ibid.*, p. 17.

[3] Except for the special case of government intervention, wages are likely to be held below the value of workers' marginal product only if the employer possesses *monopsonistic** or *oligopsonistic power**—that is, is one of a very limited number of employers of a particular type of labour with the power to force wages down below their competitive level. Such power is rare, and there is no reason to suppose that it is particularly likely to be found in engineering. In any case, the high private rate of return to engineering degrees is difficult to square with the belief that engineers are underpaid.

[4] In his essay 'The Methodology of Positive Economics', in M. Friedman, *Essays in Positive Economics*, Chicago: University of Chicago Press, 1953.

[5] See J. M. Oliver and J. R. Turton, 'Is there a shortage of skilled labour?', *British Journal of Industrial Relations*, Vol. 20, No. 2, 1982, pp. 195-200.

whom they are willing to pay more.[1] Faced with a large number of applicants for jobs, employers typically prefer the better-qualified. Over time, competition amongst applicants leads to higher and higher qualifications being offered, and in order to 'ration' jobs, employers raise the standards they require correspondingly. Jobs which you could have obtained 20 years ago with 'O' levels now require 'A' levels or even degrees if you are to have a chance of getting them—even though the skills required have actually changed very little. This is what American educationalists call 'credentialism'.

On this view, the human capital model may still be a useful explanation of individual behaviour. The private rate of return on investment in general training and education may be high (it enhances your chances of obtaining a well-paid job). The social rate of return may, however, be negligible: the economy's 'need' for qualifications is spurious.

Critics of this view argue that it implies a permanent excess of applicants over jobs. How can this be? In a free market, would wages not fall to bring demand and supply into balance? There are numerous possible responses to this. One is that employers may wish to maintain a pool of applicants, keeping wages above market-clearing levels, because of the effect of this situation on worker motivation. If unemployment is a consequence of losing a job, employees will work harder and more productively than if they could easily obtain another job at the going wage-rate.[2]

An interesting implication of such a model (and one which seems consonant with experience) is that fluctuations in the demand for labour will be manifested in variations in hiring standards (levels of education and training demanded) as well as, or instead of, variations in pay. It also seems compatible with the

[1] Here we concentrate on employers' demands for previously acquired skills. There is, however, another aspect of screening which is worth stressing. Where employers provide their own training to new applicants, this may be a cheap way of trying out potential employees in order to assess their potential in a way which interviews and other techniques cannot. Typically, such trainees have to reach some standard by the end of a course of training in order to graduate to permanent employment status, and an element of wastage can be built into employers' calculations. Thus they reduce the risk of taking on unsatisfactory workers on a permanent basis.

[2] It is also possible to link this discussion with the theory of *internal labour markets** (where workers do not compete with 'outsiders' but develop careers within one firm): 'under internal labour market régimes in many large corporations experience-pay profiles may diverge from experience-productivity profiles'. (D. Metcalf, *The Economics of Vocational Training: Past Evidence and Future Considerations, op. cit.*, p. 125.)

evidence that many workers are over-qualified for the jobs they fill.[1]

Even if this view of the market for skills is an exaggerated one, there is just sufficient in it to cast further doubt on the arguments of those who insist that general skills—and, in particular, formal certificated skills—are inadequately provided by the market and require government subsidies to their provision.

Training and Market Imperfections

Finally, before we leave these general theoretical points, it is worth noting something which propagandists of training rarely mention: that distortions created by interference with markets may actually generate a *higher* level of training than is optimal. How could this come about?

One case could arise where government legislation creates a demand for training where it would not otherwise occur. For example, the *Training in Britain* study showed health and safety and other legislation to be the second most common cause of enhanced training, with 36 per cent of respondents giving this as a reason why they were training more than they would otherwise have done.[2] While health and safety, and indeed many other types of legislation, may produce substantial net benefits to society, it is possible to imagine circumstances where legislation can create disproportionately costly training and retraining requirements. Frequent changes in taxation and auditing re-quirements, for example, might have such an effect.

Another possibility arises where employees are able to use their collective muscle to enforce unnecessary training require-ments on employers in order to keep out competition. In the public sector, 15 per cent of *Training in Britain* respondents gave trade union agreements as a reason for extra training. This may

[1] One recent study of the American labour market found that around 40 per cent of male workers reported themselves as over-educated for the jobs they performed (N. Sicherman, '"Overeducation" in the labor market', *Journal of Labour Economics*, April 1991, pp. 101-22). Although the UK position may be somewhat different, it would be surprising if substantial numbers were not similarly over-qualified here. Some would argue that women workers, who often return to jobs after having children at much lower rates of pay than before, may be even more over-educated. Joan Payne ('Training Women: Private or Public Responsibility?', *Policy Studies*, Summer 1991) points out that of women with degrees, only one-third work in professional or managerial rôles, and that one in 10 of those with A-levels work in semi- or unskilled jobs.

[2] *Training in Britain: Employers' Activities*, London: HMSO, 1989, pp. 38-39. The most important influence (reported by 56 per cent of respondents) was the 'need to sharpen competitiveness'.

be one reason why public sector employers typically provide longer periods of training, for a greater proportion of the workforce, than is the case in the private sector.

Training as a 'barrier to entry' may well exist in a number of professions, as well as in industries where trade unions have historically been powerful. This is particularly likely to be the case in occupations such as medicine and the law, which have had protected status for generations.

In these cases, high levels of training in a category of employment may not be a sign of health, but rather a sign that unnecessary costs are being imposed on employers.

Another possibility of over-provision of training arises if some part of training has in reality little to do with enhancing productivity (at least directly) but is largely a form of 'perk'. Luxurious training establishments, visits to conferences in far-flung locations, opportunities for secondments and so on may be a valuable enhancement to the quality of life of employees (including senior management), though they add little to profitability. If this is true, it is perhaps not surprising that such 'discretionary expenditures' are amongst the first to be cut in recessions.[1] While such uses of company funds to boost some of the non-wage elements of employee remuneration are perfectly legitimate, and may serve a useful function in maintaining staff morale, they may be artificially encouraged since, unlike other forms of 'pay', they are not normally subject to taxation.

[1] This suggestion may also shed some light on the observation that 'four out of every five establishments in Great Britain make no attempt to assess the benefits that they gain from undertaking training'. (*Training in Britain: Employers' Activities, ibid.*, p. 46.)

IV. TRAINING IN THE UK AND ELSEWHERE

Our examination of some of the theoretical issues raised by training suggests the possibility of market failures, but also some scepticism about their nature and extent. We now turn to examine the evidence on training provision.

Obtaining precise information about the extent and nature of training in the UK is difficult. One problem is how to classify post-compulsory education; as the Training Agency puts it,

> 'both education and training . . . help the individual to acquire skills of wide applicability . . . the actual content of education can also have varying degrees of applicability to work'.[1]

Another problem is that 'the boundary between work experience and training is equally unclear . . . training includes on-the-job experience'.[2]

Post-Compulsory Education

A quick snapshot impression of the scope of post-compulsory education can be obtained from Table 4. The Table collates

TABLE 4

NUMBERS IN POST-COMPULSORY EDUCATION
(THOUSANDS) AND PARTICIPATION RATES (%):
UK HOME STUDENTS, 1988/89

	Age					
	16	17	18	16-18	19-20	21-24
Full-time and Sandwich	448	316	168	932	265	186
	(54·8)	(35·9)	(19·4)	(36·4)	(14·7)	(4·9)
Part-time	200	183	146	529	255	545
	(24·4)	(20·9)	(16·8)	(20·6)	(14·2)	(14·3)
All F/T and P/T	648	499	314	1,461	520	731
	(79·2)	(56·8)	(36·2)	(57·0)	(28·9)	(19·2)

Source: Training Statistics 1991.

[1] Department of Employment, *Training Statistics*, London: HMSO, 1990, p. 9.
[2] *Ibid.*

[37]

TABLE 5

HIGHEST QUALIFICATION HELD BY SEX AND AGE FOR PEOPLE OF WORKING AGE: GREAT BRITAIN, SPRING 1990

(*Per cent*)

Qualification		16-19	20-24	25-34	35-44	45-64 M 45-59 F	All
Degree or	M	—	6·3	13·3	14·5	9·9	10·4
equivalent	F	—	5·2	9·4	7·9	4·1	6·1
	All	—	5·8	11·4	11·2	7·4	8·4
Higher education below degree level	M	*	4·6	5·6	5·7	4·4	4·6
	F	*	4·6	7·3	9·7	8·0	7·1
	All	0·4	4·6	6·4	7·7	5·9	5·8
GCE A level	M	20·4	38·5	36·6	36·3	31·5	33·7
or	F	16·6	29·5	17·0	13·7	9·0	15·6
equivalent	All	18·6	34·1	26·8	25·0	21·6	25·0
GCE O level	M	41·9	19·1	13·7	9·4	6·4	13·5
or	F	46·5	30·7	28·2	19·4	12·4	23·7
equivalent	All	44·2	24·8	20·9	14·4	9·0	18·4
Other	M	8·3	12·4	10·7	9·2	9·6	10·2
	F	10·0	14·8	13·5	12·2	12·8	12·8
	All	9·1	13·6	12·1	10·7	11·0	11·5
None/don't	M	29·0	18·9	20·0	24·9	38·1	27·7
know/no	F	26·3	15·2	24·6	37·0	53·7	34·7
reply	All	27·7	17·0	24·3	30·9	44·9	31·0

*Insignificant.

Source: *Labour Force Survey*, 1990 (Preliminary estimates).

statistics of those enrolled on educational courses in schools, colleges and universities up to the age of 24, and captures the bulk of those engaged in further education before, or shortly after, entering the labour force.

Table 4 does not include the 2·4 million mature (25+) students engaged in further study which swell the total in post-compulsory education to around 5 million. To put all this in a dynamic context, it should be pointed out that both the proportions staying on in education post-16 and entering higher education have risen sharply in the last three or four years.

Formal educational qualifications resulting from study are rising over time. At the most basic level, the proportion of boys leaving school with at least one 'O' level or equivalent rose from 43 per cent in 1970-71 to 54 per cent in 1987-88, while the number of girls with such a qualification rose from 44 per cent to 62 per cent over the same period. Table 5 takes a slightly different perspective by indicating the highest educational qualification achieved by those of different ages in 1990. It shows how very different are the educational achievements of younger and older cohorts in the population, and again illustrates the startling improvement in the qualifications of young females.

Training Received at Work

The Department of Employment's *Training in Britain* study, which mostly refers to 1986/87, provides some useful evidence on the training received by those in employment. Table 6 shows that, on average, employees[1] received seven days' training per year, equally split between on-the-job and off-the-job activities. The Table shows that service sector employers provided rather more training than those in manufacturing, and that the public sector provided markedly more training than the private sector, areas such as health and education being the most generous.

Data from the same source are used in the analysis of the proportions receiving training by size of establishment, shown in Table 7 for establishments where such a breakdown was possible. The broad picture emerging is that larger firms are more likely to provide training than smaller firms.[2]

More up-to-date evidence from the Labour Force Survey indicates the distribution by age of those receiving training in a four-week period in the Spring of 1990. This is shown in Table 8.

In addition to formal training, there is evidence that a good deal of informal training takes place, instituted both by employers and employees. Table 9, which draws on data from the British Social Attitudes Survey 1987, gives examples. It can be seen from the Table that this informal activity shows a similar pattern to that displayed by formal training: it declines with age.

---

[1] These figures exclude those employers with less than 10 employees.

[2] In some very large firms data were supplied by Head Offices and could not be broken down by establishment size. In these firms the average percentage receiving training was higher than the figures shown in the Table, at 61·5 per cent.

TABLE 6

TRAINING DAYS PER EMPLOYEE:
GREAT BRITAIN, 1986-87

Sector/Industry	Training days per employee		
	Total	On-job	Off-job
Total	7·0	3·4	3·6
Total Mfg.—Private	5·4	2·3	3·1
Total Services—Private	6·6	3·9	2·7
Total Private Sector	6·1	3·2	2·9
Total Public Sector	9·0	3·9	5·1
Extraction/Energy/Water	7·0	3·2	3·8
Mf. of Minerals & Chemicals	5·1	2·5	2·6
Mechanical Engineering	6·3	2·5	3·8
Electrical Engineering	7·3	2·7	4·6
Metal Goods	6·2	2·4	3·8
Textiles/Clothing	3·8	1·9	1·9
Other Processing	4·0	2·2	1·8
Construction	5·8	1·9	3·9
Transport/Communication	3·9	1·9	2·0
Wholesale	4·1	2·5	1·6
Retail	8·3	5·4	2·9
Finance/Business Services	8·0	4·4	3·6
Catering/Recreational/ Personal Services	6·2	3·6	2·7
Health	17·6	4·7	12·9
Central Government	8·5	4·0	4·5
Local Government	4·9	1·0	3·9
Education	9·6	6·8	2·8

Source: *Training in Britain: Employers' Activities*, London: HMSO, 1989.

There is, then, a very substantial amount of training undertaken in the UK. The Training Agency has estimated that the overall cost of training in Britain in 1986/87 was £33 billion, made up as shown in Table 10. This is a very substantial commitment of resources to training in Britain[1] (for comparison, the UK's Gross Domestic Product in 1986 was just under £330 billion). The claim is, however, that this commitment is still inadequate.

[1] That is, excluding Northern Ireland.

TABLE 7

EMPLOYEES RECEIVING TRAINING
BY SIZE OF ESTABLISHMENT:
GREAT BRITAIN, 1986-87*

Number of Employees in Establishment	Percentage Receiving any Training
10-24	38·1
25-49	38·3
50-99	42·6
100-199	39·9
200-499	43·4
500-999	40·9
1,000+	47·8

*Does not cover establishments with less than 10 employees or those firms where breakdown by establishment was not possible.

Source: Training in Britain: Employers' Activities, London: HMSO, 1989.

Inadequate Amounts of Training?

The belief that this country 'undertrains' has become widespread. What grounds are there for this belief?

One is the number of firms which do not appear to provide training. But should all firms train? It is not self-evident. As I argued earlier, if training is looked upon as investing in human

TABLE 8

TRAINING RECEIVED BY EMPLOYEES
IN THE LAST FOUR WEEKS:
BY AGE, GREAT BRITAIN, SPRING 1990

Employees receiving training as percentage of all employees in age group	Age					All of working age*
	16-19	20-24	25-34	35-49	50-64*	
On-the-job training only	5·2	5·5	4·7	4·1	2·7	4·3
Off-the-job training only	12·9	10·9	10·1	8·2	4·4	8·7
Both on- and off-the-job	7·1	4·1	2·1	1·8	0·7	2·4
All receiving training	25·2	20·5	16·9	14·2	7·8	15·4

*Men under 65, women under 60.

Source: Employment Gazette, April 1991.

TABLE 9

INFORMAL TRAINING OF EMPLOYEES BY AGE AND SEX
(percentages of category)

In the last two years, the respondent has:	18-24	25-34	35-44	45-54	55-64	All	M	F
Read things to learn about work	47	48	49	39	30	44	46	41
Been given special talks or lectures	46	45	44	37	32	41	44	38
Been taught by someone while working	70	42	31	20	13	36	32	40
Been placed with more experienced people to see how work should be done	65	36	24	17	14	31	29	33
Been asked to do anything just for practice	45	36	27	22	15	30	27	32
Been sent on courses to learn new methods	26	28	29	15	15	24	27	20
Been round to different parts of the organisation	33	24	24	16	17	23	25	20

Source: Training Statistics, London: HMSO, 1990.

capital, analogous to investing in plant and machinery, it is unclear why all firms should invest heavily. As with physical capital, some processes and products are less 'human capital-intensive' than others. Just as some firms do not require much physical capital, so firms operating in some fields do not require large amounts of human capital; unskilled labour and/or capital equipment may be used relatively more intensively.

Even where trained labour is required, it does not follow that the firm itself should provide the training; nobody argues that all firms should construct their own equipment or even, more pertinently, buy it outright. Leasing equipment is common-place in industry. There are clear *economies of scale** in the training

TABLE 10

OVERALL COSTS OF TRAINING IN BRITAIN, 1986/87

Source	Category	Total* (£ billion)
Individuals	Direct Expenditure (fees, etc.)	0·5
	Earnings Forgone	9·0
	Maintenance Income (deducted)	−1·0
Government	Subsidies to training and education providers	4·0
	Grants/fees support	1·5
	Maintenance support	1·5
Employers	Private sector with 10 or more employees	9·0
	Private sector with less than 10 employees	2·0
	Public sector employees	5·0
	Armed services	2·0
Total		33·0

*All figures rounded to nearest £0·5 billion.

Source: The Training Agency, *Training in Britain*, London: HMSO, 1989.

of specialists which small to moderately-sized firms cannot exploit.

Moreover, small firms in particular are often founded by mature professionals or other skilled workers operating on their own account with a handful of support staff; training may be of little relevance in such a set-up (though there are exceptions, such as tax specialists, who may have a continuing need for updating to keep pace with legislation).

A further observation is that training provision has two dimensions: *intensity* (the average amount of training provided to trainees) and *incidence* (the proportion of employees receiving training). Some industries, such as retailing, provide a little training to a large proportion of employees. Others, like engineering, offer training to a smaller proportion of employees, but for longer periods. It is unclear that we can say which is the 'better' industry from the point of view of training provision: each has different requirements.

Much has of course been made of the argument, discussed in Section III, that there is the danger of 'market failure' in the provision of general training. In particular, fear of 'poaching' of skilled labour is held to inhibit firms from providing training: if general training were provided, employees would leave for better-paid jobs elsewhere and the employers could not recapture their training costs.[1] There is, however, little evidence for this fear. The *Training in Britain* study asked firms which did not train to explain why: only 1 per cent feared that employees would leave on completion of training.[2]

Detailed examination of the provision of training by firms since 1979, using evidence from the Labour Force Survey, suggests that the pattern of training provided by firms is broadly economically rational.[3] As one would expect, older workers receive less training than younger workers (the payback period is shorter), more highly educated workers receive more training than less educated, and so on.

The incidence of employer-provided training has increased significantly in the last few years. Labour Force Survey data show 9·1 per cent of all employees had received training in the last four weeks of 1984; by 1990 this figure had reached 15·4 per cent (although the preliminary figures for 1991 show a slight downturn). Perhaps more importantly, there is also evidence that training incidence has increased fastest in areas where employment grew most rapidly (for example, jobs of a professional/technical variety). It also grew faster amongst women than amongst men, reflecting the increasing importance of female workers in the UK economy during the 1980s. Such increases appear to have occurred in both specific *and* general training, and seem to challenge the view that market failure is endemic.

---

[1] See John Stevens and Tim Walsh, 'Training and Competitiveness', in John Stevens and Robert MacKay, *Training and Competitiveness*, London: National Economic Development Office and Kogan Page, 1991, pp. 37-38.

[2] Other reasons given by establishments for not training (more than one answer could be given) included: 'static workforce, already trained' 51 per cent; 'only recruit experienced people' 42 per cent; 'work doesn't require skills' 32 per cent; 'couldn't increase responsibility' 9 per cent. (*Source*: *Training in Britain: Employers' Activities, op. cit.*, p. 53.)

[3] See C. Goodenough and G. Mavrotas, 'Workforce Training in the Thatcher Era—Market Forces and Market Failures', and F. Green, 'The Determinants of Training of Male and Female Employees in Britain', papers presented to the International Conference on the Economics of Training, Cardiff Business School, September 1991.

TABLE 11

PARTICIPATION IN EDUCATION AND TRAINING OF 16 TO 18-YEAR-OLDS: PERCENTAGE OF AGE GROUP, SELECTED COUNTRIES, 1986*

Country	Full-Time	Part-Time	All	Rank No.
Australia	50	16	66	10
Belgium	77	4	81	3
Canada	75	–	75	8
Denmark	70	6	77†	7
France	66	8	74	9
Germany	47	43	90	1
Italy	47	18	65	11
Japan	77	3	79†	5
Netherlands	77	9	86	2
Spain	52	–	52	13
Sweden	76	2	78	6
UK	**33**	**31**	**64**	**12**
USA	79	1	80	4

*or nearest available year.   †Percentages rounded in original table.

Source: Training Statistics, 1990, op. cit.

International Comparisons

Another line of argument already touched on is that the inadequacy of training in the UK is evidenced by skill shortages in key areas such as engineering. Thus in 1990 the Confederation of British Industry recorded that 28 per cent of firms in engineering and allied industries, 38 per cent of those in mechanical engineering, and 33 per cent in electrical and instrument engineering reported that their output was constrained by shortages of skilled labour. A similar pattern of reported shortages goes back for many years (it was, for example, a feature of the Finniston report of 1980),[1] and it is asserted that such shortages are much more marked than in competitor countries, notably Germany.[2]

[1] *Engineering our Future*, Cmnd. 7794, London: HMSO, 1980.

[2] Stevens and Walsh, *op. cit.*, p. 34.

TABLE 12
VOCATIONAL QUALIFICATIONS OF THE WORK-FORCE: SELECTED COUNTRIES, 1985-89
(Percentages)

	Britain	Netherlands	W. Germany	France
University degrees and higher vocational diplomas	17	18	18	14
Intermediate vocational qualifications	20	44	56	33
No vocational qualifications	63	38	26	53

Source: National Institute Economic Review, May 1992.

As indicated earlier, economists are suspicious of the notion of persistent labour shortages. Rather than search for particular instances—and the possible economic meanings—of such shortages, some commentators have relied on very broad comparisons with other countries, for example: 'Britain has fewer workers with vocational skills than any other country in the EC'.[1] What is the reality behind statements such as this?

We have already seen that international comparisons are difficult to draw. Table 11 shows a comparison for 1986 of participation in education[2] and training amongst 16 to 18-year-olds. Although the UK's position has been improving recently, its position in this 'league table' is fairly modest. However, it ought to be borne in mind that at 16, young people in the UK have already had 11 years of compulsory education, more than any other country included in the list except for the Netherlands.

Where Britain tends to show up worst in international comparisons is in terms of *formal qualifications*, which have traditionally been downplayed by British employers; and more particularly, in terms of formal *vocational* qualifications, as Table 12 illustrates.

[1] Labour Party, *Modern manufacturing strength*, London: Labour Party, February 1991, p. 13.

[2] It is worth noting that the UK devoted 4·8 per cent of its Gross National Product to publicly-funded education in 1987, a larger proportion than the USA, Japan or Germany. It seems unlikely that a major increase in public spending is a necessary condition for improving educational achievement in the UK, although the specific use to which government money should be put may be debatable.

The figures in Table 12 indicate that it is not at degree or higher diploma (HND or equivalent) level where this country is apparently at a disadvantage. Indeed, analysis of the types of degree awarded suggests that the UK's degree-level students are at least as vocationally-oriented as their counterparts overseas. The proportion of graduates whose degrees are in science and engineering is higher in the UK than in Germany or Japan, and the fastest-growing area for degree-level studies in recent years has been business studies. Continental degree programmes are often heavily academic, take much longer to complete (five to six years instead of three), have a high drop-out rate, and are characterised by outdated methods of teaching and examination.[1] They are aimed almost exclusively at full-time young people, and make little provision for part-time and mature students.

Rather, the area of apparent weakness in the UK is at intermediate and lower-level vocational qualifications—craftsmen/ women and technicians. In 1987, 12,000 craft qualifications and 18,000 technician qualifications were awarded in this country, compared with 89,000 and 45,000 respectively in West Germany. Details of the stock of qualifications held by key members of the work-force in manufacturing are given in Table 13.

The German System

Such comparisons as these have alarmed many British commentators: on the face of it, they do seem to suggest that Britain is seriously out of line with our competitors, particularly Germany. One should, however, re-emphasise that formal qualifications and skills in practice are not the same thing, and that in any case different skill 'mixes' can be used to produce the same result. As Section III showed (above, p. 20), observers such as Hart and Shipman have commented on the more direct rôle played in the production process by graduate and higher technician engineers in Britain than in Germany.[2]

Furthermore, we do need to be aware that the pattern of qualifications obtaining in Germany is not the outcome of an unaided market process, but the result of a highly regulated

---

[1] In France and Italy, for example, formal lecturing to very large groups of students is commonplace, and small-group teaching (where available) is rarely given by experienced, tenured staff. Long written examinations are virtually the only form of assessment at undergraduate level. Little attempt is made to relate the curriculum to the demands of modern life, and contacts with employers are minimal.

[2] P. E. Hart and A. Shipman, *op. cit.*

TABLE 13

QUALIFICATIONS OF TECHNICIANS
AND FOREMEN IN MANUFACTURING:
BRITAIN, FRANCE AND GERMANY*

	No vocational qualification %	Lower intermediate %	Higher intermediate %	Degree or equivalent %
Britain:				
Technicians	31	43	14	12
Foremen	55	39	3	3
France:				
Technicians	27	49	21	3
Foremen	44	51	4	1
Germany:				
Technicians	8	49	36	7
Foremen	7	29	64	–

*Britain, France: 1988; (West) Germany: 1987.

Source: H. Steedman, G. Mason and K. Wagner, 'Intermediate Skills in the Workplace: Deployment, Standards and Supply in Britain, France and Germany', *National Institute Economic Review*, May 1991.

labour market which introduces a number of potential distortions. The much-praised 'dual' system, based on formal apprenticeship and combining vocational training at the workplace with compulsory instruction in vocational schools up to the age of 19,[1] is the product of a corporatist ethic. It involves Chambers of Commerce, Land governments and trade unions, and lays down tight specifications for training for around 400 'recognised occupations'. Laws prevent the employment of young people without providing formal training (one of the reasons why the *Gastarbeiter* ('guest worker') system developed in West Germany, as indigenous young people were in effect prevented from taking low-paid, low-skilled jobs of the type which young people often perform in other countries). They also prevent people setting up, for example, handicraft workshops and other

[1] For accounts of the German system, see B. Casey, 'The Dual Apprentice System and the Recruitment and Retention of Young Persons in West Germany', *British Journal of Industrial Relations*, March 1986, and K. Wagner, 'Training Efforts and Industrial Efficiency in West Germany', in John Stevens and Robert MacKay (eds.), *Training and Competitiveness, op. cit.*

enterprises without having a *Meister* qualification, a provision which has clear anti-competitive implications.

The typical apprenticeship lasts three to three-and-a-half years. There are some shorter apprenticeships of two years' duration. Significantly, unions want longer training periods and are pressing for the abolition of two-year schemes, while employers have recently been pressing for the much wider use of shorter apprenticeships, suggesting that there may be a deliberate attempt on the part of unions to use training as a 'barrier to entry', as suggested earlier. As it is, the average age of apprentices has risen from 16·6 years in 1970 to 18·5 years in 1988, part of a more general phenomenon of increasingly delayed entry to the labour market: in some cases, young people are actually entering apprenticeships after completion of higher education. Apprentices are paid much lower wages than qualified workers (in the mid-1980s, only about one-third of adult rates).

All this makes the German training system, and the employment of young people, very different from practice and experience in the UK. However, the general admiration of the German system requires some qualification. It did not prevent higher unemployment in the 1980s than in earlier periods. Successful completion of an apprenticeship does not guarantee employment with the employer which provided the training, and some have claimed that German employers exploit the system in order to reap the benefits of cheap labour tied to the firm for several years. Many skilled workers do not in practice use the skills for which they are trained: they subsequently leave the occupation they trained for to obtain better-paid work elsewhere, even if this is sometimes at a lower skill-level.[1]

Furthermore, although much is now made of the desirability of flexibility in training, even sympathetic commentators[2] note

'an element of inflexibility in the German apprenticeship system, one that is an inevitable consequence of the high degree of regulation to which it is subject'.

One recent study, taking carefully matched samples of young British and German workers in similar labour markets, found unexpected strengths in the training experiences of young

[1] See K. Wagner, *ibid.*, p. 134.

[2] Such as Bernard Casey, 'Recent Developments in the German Apprenticeship System', *British Journal of Industrial Relations*, June 1991, p. 214.

Britons. They are introduced into real work situations much earlier than German youths, and are given greater responsibility. Higher proportions of British respondents

'reported experience of information technology, learning new skills, being challenged or tested, using their initiative, and working co-operatively in groups. In many respects the British samples appeared the more enterprising.'[1]

[1] Klaus Hurrelmann, Ken Roberts, 'Problems and Solutions', in John Brynner and Ken Roberts (eds.), *Youth and Work: transition to employment in England and Germany*, London: Anglo-German Foundation for the Study of Industrial Society, 1991, pp. 235-36.

V. TRAINING IN THE UK AND THE GOVERNMENT

I have now indicated some of the reasons why apparent market failure is held to justify government intervention in training. In this section the history of government policy towards training in the UK is surveyed from early developments, through the post-war years and up to the policies promoted by the administrations of Mrs Thatcher and Mr Major. Several key areas which the Government has recently chosen to emphasise are then examined.

Beginnings

There were some initiatives to encourage technical education in the 19th century,[1] but large-scale central government involvement began with the First World War. The imperatives of wartime shortages of labour impelled the Ministry of Munitions in 1915 to pioneer training schemes for men and women to turn them rapidly into semi-skilled workers.[2] Later in the War, the Ministry of Labour began preparations for training disabled ex-servicemen, and some of those able-bodied men who had missed out on training as a result of entering war service. With the advent of peace these schemes were over-subscribed and the Ministry was obliged to offer cash grants instead of training to many of those on the waiting list.

By the mid-1920s, economic recession had created a whole new set of problems leading to a considerable expansion of government-financed training. There were five main developments:

(i) Government Training Centres, where men undertook six-month skill training courses under conditions of strict discipline;

(ii) Instructional Centres for the long-term unemployed, where men undertook hard manual labour for 12 weeks in isolated

---

[1] For example, the Technical Instruction Act of 1889, which made county councils and county boroughs responsible for technical education, funded by a diversion of 'whiskey money' and a penny rate.

[2] See J. Sheldrake and S. Vickerstaff, *The History of Industrial Training in Britain*, Aldershot: Avebury, 1987, pp. 7-9.

camps[1] in order to rehabilitate them for the rigours of employment;

(iii) Training Schemes for Women, concentrating on traditional female skills in order to equip trainees for domestic service;

(iv) Individual Vocational Training, involving payment of grants to support individual training where a strong case could be made; and

(v) Junior Instructional Centres for unemployed under-18s.

Approaching two million people passed through these schemes in the inter-war years.

All of these schemes were seen as responses to particular problems, rather than as replacements for traditional apprenticeship schemes or other means by which the private sector trained employees. Nor did the experiences of the Second World War alter matters fundamentally. Although training requirements obviously increased as labour was diverted to the war effort, the system of 'reserved occupations' prevented the chaotic stripping of the factories of skilled labour which had characterised the early stages of the First World War. The main initial requirement was for engineering workers, and later for shipbuilders and mineworkers. Government Training Centres were expanded rapidly, courses were shortened to increase the throughput, and in 1941 women and girls were admitted to these former male preserves.

But it was always clear that such training was to be a temporary expedient. Ernest Bevin, as Minister of Labour and National Service in the wartime coalition government, was keen to prevent 'dilution' of skills and the undercutting of skilled labour when peace returned. Penetration of government trainees into long-term employment was resisted by the trade unions. Management, which for much of the post-war period was to tolerate and sometimes even encourage trade unions in the belief that this brought 'order' into industrial relations, acquiesced in this return to the *status quo*.

The Post-war Years

After the War, concern about training slipped down the agenda. Government Training Centres were run down, and what

---

[1] Sheldrake and Vickerstaff (*ibid.*, p. 15) say that 'life at an Instructional Centre was rather like three months in an open prison'.

political interest was shown concentrated on the problems of young workers.[1] In the 1944 Education Act, the idea of vocational education had been a feature of the tripartite system of grammar, secondary modern and technical schools (though the latter often tended to get squeezed out in practice). In 1948 the Juvenile Employment Service was set up, but there were few further developments. By 1959 the Crowther Report[2] was again calling for improved education for those not academically inclined.

The 1950s were a buoyant period for the British economy, but by the early 1960s there was a widespread awareness of Britain's relative decline as other countries recovered from the War. This was the period of 'stop-go' in macro-economic policy, and it was argued that skill shortages were one of the factors constraining the economy in periods of boom. By 1962 the Conservative government, at the height of its enthusiasm for corporatist economic planning, was publishing a White Paper[3] calling for improvements in the quality and extent of provision of training, and arguing for the expense of training to be spread by a levy system on employers. The Industrial Training Act was passed in March 1964, setting up the Central Training Council (including six employer and six trade union representatives) and making provision for tripartite Industrial Training Boards (ITBs) to manage the new system of grants and levies for training.

Industrial Training Boards grew rapidly; by May 1966, 7·5 million workers were in industries covered by them. But from the beginning there were criticisms, which by the end of the decade had produced a consensus that the Act had failed in its objectives. One line of criticism came from small firms, which paid the levy and had to deal with an increasing amount of paperwork, but were often unable to claim grants back because they could not spare workers for the off-the-job training which the ITBs emphasised. The unions, by contrast, thought the powers of the Central Training Council were too limited and called for a greater element of central direction plus an extension of the Training Board system throughout industry. Other criticisms included the view that there was too much duplication,

---

1 And, to a lesser extent, marginal groups such as the disabled and the 'hard to place'—a 'social welfare' rather than a 'manpower needs' approach.

2 Central Advisory Council for Education (England): *15 to 18* (The Crowther Report: Chairman, Lord Crowther), Vols. I and II, London: HMSO, 1959.

3 *Industrial Training: Government Proposals*, Cmnd. 1892, London: HMSO, 1962.

with each ITB funding training in skills common across industry. The Donovan Commission[1] took the view in 1968 that many of the skills problems in British industry arose from restrictive practices and the traditional narrow systems of apprenticeship which gave raise to them; these had not been tackled by the ITBs. By 1971 the Confederation of British Industry was calling for exemption of small firms from the levy and an emphasis on retraining to promote greater labour market flexibility.[2]

It was against this background that the Heath administration set up the Manpower Services Commission (MSC) to play an active rôle at the national level in promoting labour market efficiency in general and improved training in particular. Direct government training, through the Training Opportunities Scheme (TOPs), was to be expanded, with a focus on general, transferable skills.

Over the next few years the MSC proved unable to develop a significant re-orientation of training at the national level, tending rather to react to events. It was during this period that rising unemployment forced the government to respond by developing the series of *ad hoc* initiatives which was the precursor of the jungle of job creation and training schemes that was to be a feature of the 1980s.

Government Training Policy Since 1979

The election of a Conservative administration in 1979 might have been expected to lead to a cutback in spending on programmes such as those funded by the MSC, but this was not to be the case. On the contrary, total spending rose considerably, as Table 14 indicates.[3] This was partly an almost inevitable consequence of the recession of the early 1980s, when unemployment rose to unprecedented post-war levels and youth unemployment in particular was seen as a major socio-economic problem. But it was also in part the result of a genuine conviction that here was one field where, contrary to other areas of

[1] *Trade Unions and Employers' Associations: Report of the Royal Commission, 1965-1968* (Chairman: The Rt. Hon. Lord Donovan), Cmnd. 3623, London: HMSO, 1968.

[2] See Sheldrake and Vickerstaff, *op. cit.*, p. 41.

[3] Note that this Table only covers central government expenditure through the Manpower Services Commission and its successors. Local authority spending on colleges and student grants, plus central government spending on higher education, brought the total costs of government-funded training and education to £7 billion in 1986-87.

TABLE 14

CENTRAL GOVERNMENT SPENDING ON TRAINING AND ENTERPRISE, 1978-79 TO 1990-91

Year	Training (current prices, £m.)[1]	Enterprise (current prices, £m.)	Total (current prices, £m.)	Total (1990-91 prices, £m.)
1978-79	377·3	—	377·3	940·5
1979-80	464·2	—	464·2	991·3
1980-81	576·0	—	576·0	1,038·5
1981-82	764·6	—	764·6	1,256·6
1982-83	882·8	2·4	885·2	1,356·5
1983-84	1,064·6	23·2	1,087·8	1,593·7
1984-85	1,159·2	80·1	1,239·3	1,728·6
1985-86	1,278·0	108·4	1,386·4	1,834·5
1986-87	1,461·6	154·8	1,616·4	2,071·2
1987-88	1,633·6	204·0	1,837·6	2,235·9
1988-89	2,042·9	203·3	2,276·4	2,581·4
1989-90[2]	2,669·5	184·4	2,853·9	3,038·8
1990-91[3]	2,704·5	148·6	2,853·1	2,853·1

[1] Includes Youth Opportunities Programme, 1978-84.
[2] Forecast Outturn.   [3] Estimated Provision.

Source: Training Statistics, 1990.

economic policy in which the government sought to disengage itself, increased government action was called for.

MSC Chairman, David Young (later, as Lord Young, a Cabinet Minister), was a strong advocate of creating a 'Training Culture'. The New Training Initiative of 1981 was one of the first fruits of this enthusiasm; it led to the foundation of the Youth Training Scheme (YTS), initially a one-year programme, later expanded into a two-year scheme and made virtually compulsory for unemployed school leavers.[1] Other developments included the introduction of many vocational courses into schools and colleges—for example, the Technical and Vocational Initiative, the Certificate in Pre-Vocational Education, and the 'Enterprise schemes' in polytechnics and universities.

[1] A point discussed in more detail below (pp. 59-60).

TABLE 15

NUMBERS OF STARTS ON ADULT
AND YOUTH PROGRAMMES, 1978-79 AND 1988-89

Scheme	Numbers: 1978-79	Numbers: 1988-89
Community Industry	6,700	10,800
Community Programme	19,700	84,000
Enterprise Allowance Scheme	–	98,500
Youth Opps Programme	162,200	–
Voluntary Projects Programme	–	88,200
Youth Training Scheme	–	407,500
Training Opps Programme	70,200	–
Ind Language Training Scheme	–	17,200
Job Training Scheme – Old	–	24,300
Job Training Scheme – New	–	50,700
Training for Enterprise	–	89,800
Local Grants to Employers	–	106,800
Self-standing Work Preparation	–	27,900
Training Linked to Community Programme	–	16,600
Employment Training	–	238,600
National Priority Skills Scheme	–	2,100
Total	258,800	1,263,000

Source: Training Statistics, 1990.

Some idea of the range of training and enterprise programmes available in 1988-89, compared with 1978-79, together with numbers, can be obtained from Table 15, though this excludes many developments in schools and colleges.[1]

But alongside the expansion of government-funded training, many institutional changes were introduced. The Manpower Services Commission became the Training Commission, then

[1] It also excludes a number of schemes which were born and died between these two dates, for example Business Training, Access to Information Technology and the Open Tech Programme. One day, no doubt, an historian will disinter the details of all these schemes.

the Training Agency, many of the functions of which have recently been devolved to the new Training and Enterprise Councils (TECs). While the MSC was a product of 1970s corporatism, this is definitely not so for the TECs. Most of the Industry Training Boards were scrapped in 1981, and the funding of the others removed. Trade unions were *personae non gratae* in training circles in the 1980s, although some have detected a slight softening of the line recently. Training is now seen as primarily a responsibility of employers, who dominate the TECs, despite the huge sums of public money still invested in it.

It was hoped that the numbers on, and costs of, government training schemes would fall sharply over the next few years, but the early 1990s recession has tempered this optimism. The publication of the 1991 White Paper[1] showed that the Conservatives had not lost their enthusiasm for innovation in training. I shall examine some aspects of its proposals shortly. First, however, something general must be said about government training schemes of the sort listed in Table 15.

Evaluating Training Schemes

In the worst years of the recession of the early 1980s, many of these schemes had minimal training content (the unpopular Youth Opportunities Programme,[2] for instance), though more recently determined efforts have been made to improve the quality of training provision. Great hope was placed in the devolution of funding from the Training Agency to the TECs, though I shall suggest below that this policy may bring problems of its own.

There is still plenty of room for improvement. In 1988-89, only 42 per cent of young people leaving the two-year YTS programme obtained a qualification to show for their time. In the following year less than 10 per cent of those completing the new adult Employment Training Scheme gained a vocational qualification. For 1991-92 the rechristened Youth Training expected 75 per cent of its leavers to have gained a qualification; Employment Training planned for 20 per cent to have qualified.

[1] *Education and Training for the 21st Century*, Cm. 1536, London: HMSO, May 1991.

[2] First introduced in 1978 to provide temporary placements for unemployed school-leavers, the programme had some initial credibility, but it was swamped by the rise in unemployment in the early 1980s. By mid-1981 only about 40 per cent of trainees were finding a permanent job.

In both cases, however, the qualifications to be gained were at a fairly low level, NVQs 1 or 2.[1]

Of course it could be argued that the purpose of these schemes has been to make people employable rather than to have achieved paper qualifications, and that in this respect their performance appears more impressive. For example, in 1989-90 just over two-thirds of those completing YTS went into a job, while another 15 per cent went into further education and training. Such figures, however, provide little indication of the success of a training programme. For one thing, 'first destinations' are a very limited indicator of future career prospects. As one economist has written:

> 'for programmes . . . where longer-term supply performance effects are more important, much of the evaluation needs to be done several years after trainees have completed the scheme'.[2]

Yet in practice such evaluation is rarely carried out. It is expensive and time-consuming to conduct follow-up studies, say, three to five years after completion of training. Politicians with short electoral horizons cannot or will not wait for answers. In any case, the pace of innovation in training in recent years has been such that delayed answers which cast doubt on the efficacy of schemes can usually be dismissed as relating to an earlier mode of the scheme which has been replaced by a more effective version.

Even where the political will exists to conduct serious research into the effectiveness of government training, the practical difficulties are considerable. What we wish to know is how a scheme improves the job prospects of trainees. We should compare training outcomes with what would have happened in the absence of training.

Ideally, we would conduct an experiment, randomly assigning one group of people to the training programme and the other (the 'control group') to non-participation. We would then compare the effect of the training on individuals' probability of obtaining jobs (or whatever other indicator of success is regarded as appropriate). In practice this cannot be done. On many programmes, places may be available in principle to all comers; on others they may may be rationed on a first-come-first-served

[1] See below, pp. 66-70.

[2] J. Stern, *Methods of Analysis of Public Expenditure Programmes with Employment Objectives*, Government Economic Service Working Paper No. 103, London: HM Treasury, May 1988, p. 13.

basis. In neither case can you compel individuals to take part in a particular programme, though you can provide incentives for them to join.

In reality, those entering a scheme are unlikely to be a random selection of the potentially eligible. On some schemes those who take up places are likely to be more intelligent and enterprising than the average; on others, places may be overwhelmingly taken by low achievers. Thus researchers require detailed data on individuals' life histories, attitudes, family background, and so on, in order to distinguish the effects of training from other factors. Although there are some datasets which provide such information on individuals, they are never perfect and much depends on the skill and ingenuity of the researcher and the appropriateness of the original data, often collected for an entirely different purpose.

Another serious problem with measuring the effectiveness of training schemes for the unemployed is that they create incentives for employers to behave differently than they would otherwise have done. This aggravates the difficulty of discerning the effects of a programme. For instance, where employers are paid by the government to take on trainees, there are commonly *displacement effects**, where the introduction of trainees reduces employment opportunities which would otherwise have been available.[1]

Youth Training

Moving from these general considerations to the particular, I now turn to the biggest of the Government's schemes. The Youth Training Scheme (now renamed Youth Training) grew out of earlier schemes: in particular, the Youth Opportunities Programme, which was primarily a work experience and 'orientation' scheme for young school-leavers.

The YTS, which replaced it in 1983, had a significantly stronger emphasis on training. It expanded to cover nearly all 16 to 18-year-olds not in full-time education, including those with formal contracts of employment or apprenticeships. For the latter it became a straight subsidy to the employer. Initially a

[1] Displacement effects can be subdivided into *deadweight loss** (where employers substitute programme trainees for, say, apprentices they would otherwise have taken on, so that in effect the firm's training bill is paid for by the government and there is no net increase in training), and the *substitution effect** (where trainees substitute for some other group of workers—for example, part-timers or older workers—and unemployment is created elsewhere).

one-year programme, it was expanded to two years in 1985. With the removal of benefits from 16 to 18-year-olds, the scheme became virtually compulsory for young unemployed people. By the late 1980s, 40 per cent or more of young people were spending at least some time on a YTS programme; it had become a rite of passage comparable to National Service for older generations. Central government funding for the scheme amounted to a billion pounds a year.

The orientation of the scheme is changing. Training and Enterprise Councils have taken over the rôle of placing contracts for Youth Training places from the Training Agency. Experiments with Training Credits[1] have been sufficiently successful for the principle to be extended. Pressure is growing for training to lead to formal qualifications. However, Youth Training looks set to remain as the main means by which our youngest school-leavers (i.e., excluding those who stay on in education) enter the labour market.

A quiet revolution has therefore occurred over the last decade in the means by which young people are introduced to the job market. It amounts almost to a 'nationalisation' of much initial training. Its objectives, methods and implications, however, have not been been widely discussed by the general public— certainly not as widely as recent changes in the formal education system have been. This may reflect the fact that few of the children of middle-class opinion-formers enter Youth Training.

Some attempts have been made to evaluate its success. We should discount government claims about the numbers of jobs scheme leavers obtain: many would presumably have obtained jobs anyway, particularly after the lapse of time involved in a one- or two-year scheme. One indicator of success might be formal qualifications obtained. Here the record has not been particularly impressive. In 1987-88 only 29 per cent of leavers obtained a qualification, though we have seen that this proportion is projected to rise sharply.

Objective evaluation of YTS so far is very difficult; the scheme has changed so much that evaluation inevitably refers to older versions of the scheme. If these are shown not to be

---

[1] Training credits are vouchers which enable young people to 'buy' training from providers approved by Training and Enterprise Councils. Following pilot schemes in a small number of areas, the principle is now to be spread more widely. The White Paper, *People, Jobs and Opportunity*, Cm. 1810, London: HMSO, 1992, included a target for every young person leaving full-time education in 1996 to be offered a training credit.

successful, defenders of Youth Training are likely to respond that things have changed for the better.

Ideally, training schemes should be evaluated, as already indicated, by comparing those engaged on a scheme with a 'control group' of similar individuals who did not participate. In practice this was never feasible for YTS; given its origins in a period of very high youth unemployment, it was not acceptable to deny places to a group of individuals in order to provide a matched sample. Thus non-experimental methods, employing *multiple regression techniques**, are necessary in order to separate out the effects of YTS from other influences on an individual's success in the labour market.[1] (Even these methods are applicable only where there are large numbers of both participants and non-participants; as the scheme has grown in coverage this is no longer the case.)

In one study, Brian Main and Michael Shelly[2] used data from the Scottish Young People's Survey to examine the pay and labour market status in April 1986 of those who left school in the Summer of 1984. They found that having participated in YTS made a statistically significant improvement to an individual's probability of being in a job, though the effect (at about 15 percentage points) was small in relation to that from having achieved good school exam results and was often outweighed by the negative effect of a disadvantaged family background. There was no statistically significant effect on earnings.

In a later study examining the achievements of these young people in October 1987, Main again found a statistically significant improvement in employment probability, of the same magnitude.[3] Main, however, now made the interesting discovery that it appeared to be the fact of having participated which was significant, not having completed the scheme. He concluded from this that YTS was acting as a 'screening device' for

[1] The problem with such approaches is that there is no universally agreed method which should be used in these exercises. Differences in estimation techniques can lead to wide variation in estimates of the effects of training schemes, so much so that one study reports 'considerable pessimism about the utility of non-experimental methods of assessing program impacts'. (W. C. Riddell, 'Evaluation of Manpower and Training Programs: the North American Experience', University of British Columbia, Department of Economics, *Discussion Paper*, No. 90-19, 1990, p. 58.) Some experts are, however, more optimistic.

[2] Brian G. M. Main and Michael A. Shelly, 'The Effectiveness of the Youth Training Scheme as a Manpower Policy', *Economica*, Vol. 57, November 1990, pp. 495-514.

[3] Brian G. M. Main, 'The effect of the Youth Training Scheme on employment probability', *Applied Economics*, Vol. 23, February 1991, pp. 367-72.

employers, enabling them to select promising employees, rather than that training provided an increase in skills of direct value to the employer.

Careful studies such as these suggest that YTS has been modestly successful in improving the job prospects of participants, though there is an indication that it may not be necessary for the scheme to last for two years to achieve this result (particularly where no qualification is achieved). It is also true that there are substantial displacement effects from Youth Training. In an early study, B. M. Deakin and Cliff Pratten[1] found that the effects varied with establishment size, from 28 to 49 per cent in the case of the deadweight loss effect and from 2 to 20 per cent in the case of the substitution effect. Estimates reported by Chapman and Tooze from the Dundee and Renfrew area suggested a rather higher displacement effect.[2] Later work by Begg, Blake and Deakin reinforced this view: they found that the displacement rate increased over time, reaching 80 per cent by 1989 (divided between 71 per cent deadweight and 9 per cent substitution effects).[3]

The implication of these findings, let it be clear, is that a substantial proportion of the public money going to finance Youth Training is funding training which the private sector would otherwise have paid for itself.

The Trouble with TECs

Responsibility for programmes such as Youth Training is now devolved to the Training and Enterprise Councils. TECs are 'employer-led, independent local bodies whose aim ... [is] to foster economic growth and regeneration'.[4] There are 82 in England and Wales and 22 equivalent Local Enterprise Companies (LECs) in Scotland (Northern Ireland, as in so many other ways, is treated differently).

1 B. M. Deakin and C. F. Pratten, 'Economic Effects of YTS', *Employment Gazette*, October 1987.

2 P. G. Chapman and M. J. Tooze, 'Some Economic Implications of the Youth Training Scheme', *Royal Bank of Scotland Review*, September 1987, pp. 14-23. Chapman and Tooze also express 'serious reservations' about the occupational distribution of Youth Training places. At the time their research was conducted, 45 per cent of all places nationally were in clerical/administration or retail 'occupational training families'. As they point out, such a pattern does not fit well with the distribution of full-time jobs to which young people are aspiring.

3 I. G. Begg, A. P. Blake and B. M. Deakin, 'YTS and the Labour Market', *British Journal of Industrial Relations*, June 1991, pp. 223-36.

4 *Labour Market Quarterly Report*, Training Agency, February 1990, p. 10.

They have been welcomed by private industry, but also by the Labour and Liberal Democrat parties (which would, however, like to see some redirection of the TECs' efforts). Over 1,200 board members have been recruited, mainly company chairmen and women and chief executives (though in some regions of the country job definitions have had to be more elastic than elsewhere).

Their main task has been to take over from the Training Agency the allocation of the well over £2 billion of taxpayers' money which is devoted to training and enterprise schemes (primarily Youth Training and Employment Training). More generally, they are intended to promote a 'training culture' throughout industry and close the perceived 'skills gap' between the UK and its competitors. The TECS are not training providers themselves: they form contracts for the provision of training with industry boards, private employers, public and voluntary bodies and private training consultancies.

The inspiration for the TECs seems to have come from the United States—and, in particular, from Boston's Private Industry Councils.[1] They represent a break with both the corporatist tradition of the post-war period (no direct trade union, industry association or local authority involvement) and with the much older tradition of centralised Whitehall control of public spending (decisions are to be taken locally rather than nationally). It is argued that local business people, the ultimate employers of the trainees whose funding they are to oversee, are better-equipped to make judgements about training than civil servants.

All to the good, perhaps. But there are a number of question-marks about TECs. One is the long-term feasibility of placing the direction of training in the hands of part-time, unpaid top executives with many other responsibilities. Once the first flush of energy has died down and TECs settle into a routine, attendance at council and committee meetings is likely to become a chore rather than an enthusiasm. In any case, the practicalities of busy TECs must be that their Chief Executives and staff (mainly seconded from the Training Agency) will in effect control the agenda. Such people are unlikely to be any more accountable than traditional civil servants.[2]

[1] See 'The training trap', *The Economist*, 21 April 1990, p. 33.

[2] Perhaps even less so. The Chief Executive of Lincolnshire TEC wrote to Tony Blair, MP (who, as employment spokesman for the official Opposition, surely had a right to ask
[*Cont'd. on p. 64*]

The Geographical Problem

Another question-mark hangs over the appropriateness of defining training requirements at the local level. One aspect of this is geographical: travel-to-work areas may not coincide with TECs' areas of responsibility. This problem arises most obviously in London, but is also present in a number of other conurbations. It creates co-ordination difficulties and potential boundary disputes. Another aspect of the problem relates to training providers. In the past, many nationally- (and internationally-) based companies, and industry-wide training boards, have provided training places for YTS and other government schemes, negotiating directly with the Training Agency or the Department of Employment. Now they are faced with having to negotiate locally with a large number of separate TECs or LECs. Apart from the additional costs in time and resources of such arrangements, firms may be unwilling to guarantee a specific number of places in one particular location. This seems to have been the reason why a number of national employers (such as Boots, Midland Bank and Mothercare) pulled out of previous arrangements. While it may be possible for a firm to guarantee 1,000 training places nationally, that is a different matter from guaranteeing 25 in Milton Keynes, 40 in Oldham, and so on.

Apart from these structural problems, there are concerns about the nature of the policies likely to be adopted by TECs. Much has been made of the contention that local employers are best-placed to know what local training requirements are. Fair enough, but some critics have pointed out that such employers have strong incentives to fund very specific training (in the sense discussed earlier) for their own needs, rather than general training, thus substituting government funds for private funds rather than swelling the total resources applied to training.[1]

Another concern has been the way in which funds are to be provided to TECs. They were initially (as a legacy of the Training Agency) provided in relation to 'needs' as measured in

questions) that 'it is quite frankly not in our business interests to use valuable staff resources in order to provide you . . . with a range of information that will only be used to score political party points'. ('Training councils "deny MP details of £1bn spending"', *The Independent*, 20 June 1991.)

[1] See, for example, 'Appraisal: Training', *National Institute Economic Review*, May 1991, where the National Institute team argue that the danger inherent in TEC control is that 'expenditure will be concentrated on training of a narrow and job-specific nature which is in the interests of existing employers, rather than general training which is in the interests of employees and perhaps of their alternative and subsequent employers' (p. 9).

[64]

unemployment—thus ignoring what many TEC members saw as the more important task of upgrading the skills of those currently in work. Future funding is planned to be 'output-related' in terms of qualifications, with funds going to those TECs which produce the highest ratio of achieved qualifications to scheme participants. The problem here is that the cheapest qualifications to prepare trainees for are the lowest grades (National Vocational Qualifications Levels 1 and 2): these bear no necessary relation to the country's long-term skills requirements, but provide more certificates per pound spent. It is also true, as Peck observes, that

> 'capital-intensive training such as engineering and computing skills will be less profitable than training which requires little capital investment, such as retailing and clerical skills'.[1]

Finally, it should be noted that the TECs already show signs of developing into a classic pressure group to lobby for public funds and effective control over training policy. They set up the independent 'Group of Ten' (G10), with a Chairman and administrative office, and are developing a permanent constitution and funding.[2] The Government was apparently so worried about this initiative that it chose to revive and expand the role of the National Training Task Force as a counterweight to the influence of G10.[3] Yet its influence has grown significantly. In unpublished papers submitted in response to the Government's *White Papers* on education and training, and discussed in a G10 session closed to press and public, they argued for effective control over the budgets of technical colleges, raising the school-leaving age to 18, and the abolition of A-levels.[4] More recently they have vociferously demanded increased public spending on training schemes, and reductions in central government insistence on auditing their activities. This is classic undemocratic pressure-group behaviour, whatever the merits or demerits of the proposals themselves.

So the advent of TECs may not be the unmitigated blessing that some supporters have claimed. Giving employers a greater rôle in public training provision has potential costs as well as benefits.

[1] J. Peck, 'Letting the market decide (with public money): Training and Enterprise Councils and the future of labour market programmes', *Critical Social Policy*, Vol. 11, No. 1, Summer 1991, p. 1.

[2] See 'Training chiefs to form industrial pressure group', *The Independent*, 5 March 1991.

[3] See 'Industry to oversee training strategy', *The Independent*, 11 April 1991.

[4] See 'Bosses bid for training purse strings', *The Guardian*, 29 July 1991.

Certifying Qualifications

Another key element in current thinking is the development of National Vocational Qualifications, to which a number of references have already been made.

We have seen that one important difference between the UK and many of our international competitors is that our labour force, particularly at the intermediate and lower skill levels, possesses fewer formal qualifications. The answer to this perceived problem has been twofold. There has been an attempt to increase the total amount of training undertaken, but also to ensure that a far higher proportion of the work-force becomes formally certificated.[1] This in turn creates an obligation to

'reform vocational qualifications and to create a framework within which they can be located, so that they are easy to understand and their relationship to further education and training opportunities is clear'.[2]

The chosen means to this end is the National Council for Vocational Qualifications (NCVQ). Set up in 1986, this body was set a range of disparate tasks in the training field, the most important of which was to rationalise the large number of vocational qualifications which had grown up in the UK and link them to the system of academic qualifications, thus 'bridging the divide' between education and training.

The NCVQ certainly set about this task with enthusiasm, arguably going beyond its brief by imposing a standard model on vocational training in this country. By the end of 1992 it is envisaged that 80 per cent of the work-force will be in jobs where the National Vocational Qualification framework is installed; ambitions are now focussing on higher professional qualifications and expansion of NVQs into full-time school-based and higher education courses, though this presents major new problems.[3]

[1] In an interesting recent paper, Eliakim Katz and Adrian Ziderman have suggested that these objectives may be in conflict. Building on Becker's distinction between 'general' and 'specific' training, discussed earlier (above, p. 24), they argue in effect that certification converts specific into general training. Since employers may, as we have seen, be more willing to provide the former than the latter, 'certification . . . limits company financed training, and places a heavier financing burden on workers'. (E. Katz and A. Ziderman, 'Investment in General Training: The Role of Information and Labour Mobility', *Economic Journal*, Vol. 100, December 1990, pp. 1,147-158.)

[2] *Education and Training for the 21st Century*, Cm. 1536, London: HMSO, May 1991, Vol. 1, p. 16.

[3] For a discussion of some of these problems, see Alison Fuller, 'Off track at the edge of a jungle', *The Times Higher Education Supplement*, 13 December 1991.

Figure 2:
The NVQ System

NVQ Level	General NVQ	Occupationally-specific NVQ	Academic Equivalent
5	Vocationally-related Post Graduate qualifications	Professional qualification middle management	–
4	Vocationally-related Degrees/Higher National Diploma	Higher technician. Junior management.	Degree
3	Vocationally-related National Diploma. Advanced Craft Preparation	Technician. Advanced Craft. Supervisor.	A/AS level
2	Broad-based Craft Foundation	Basic Craft Certificate	GCSE
1	Pre-Vocational Certificate	Semi-skilled	National Curriculum

The NVQ system is based on five levels of 'competences' or 'standards of performance' (Figure 2). The idea is that vocational qualifications should all be re-orientated to meet the specific requirements identified by employers in various occupations at these different levels. Employers are to be seen to be clearly in the lead: the approach

'requires those in employment to define the outcomes needed and those in education and training to decide what type of learning is required to lead to these outcomes'.[1]

The NVQ approach is to concentrate on defining occupational requirements in such a way that performance, rather than knowledge, is the key to achievement:

'[W]ithin a competence-based model of qualifications there is no justification for assessing knowledge for its own sake, but only for its contribution to predicting competent performance'.[2]

[1] Peter J. Thompson, 'Providing A Qualified Society To Meet The Challenge', *National Westminster Bank Quarterly Review*, February 1989, p. 24.

[2] National Vocational Qualifications Information and Guidance Notes, No. 2, May 1991.

The implication is that testing is to be work-based wherever possible, and competence has to be demonstrated in normal day-to-day performance of the job, supplemented by work simulations for those in college-based training and a limited amount of oral or written 'questioning'—the word 'examination' is downplayed—if necessary.

Where academic qualifications such as A-levels are 'norm-referenced' (and thus a proportion is guaranteed to fail), the NVQ approach has been likened to the driving test. A checklist of competences is provided, and individuals able to demonstrate satisfactory performance in each of these areas achieves the qualification. Each level is to be linked to other levels in a clear sequence, thus enabling individuals 'to plan their career paths and to see a clear ladder of progress to higher qualifications'.[1]

Will the NCVQ Approach Succeed?

The approach of the NCVQ certainly represents a radical break with the past. But how successful will it be in raising skill levels across British industry? It has been granted very considerable powers. In effect, the NCVQ now has a virtual monopoly of validation of vocational qualifications. Any qualification, of whatever previous standing (and many qualifications—those of the RSA and City and Guilds, for example—have long had high standing and international recognition), must accept the basic NCVQ philosophy or it will cease to be recognised. The consequences of this would be fatal for an examining body or institution, for all government training funds are tied to NVQ recognition.

Economists would not, as a general rule, accept that monopoly status of this sort is likely to encourage independent innovation and experimentation. Moreover, it appears that the NCVQ approach is based more on enthusiasm for a philosophy than on sound research, a point which comes out clearly in much of their literature where little attempt is made to evaluate the costs and benefits of alternative methods of competence testing.[2]

---

[1] *Education and Training for the 21st Century*, Cm. 1536, *op. cit.*, Vol. 1, p. 16.

[2] As Ron Johnson puts it: 'where is the research that underpins these programmes? There is a great deal of theorising and also a good deal of investigative studies, but these seem to fall short of the kind of research we need'. (R. Johnson, 'Training Research in France and West Germany—Its Role in the Development of Training', in J. Stevens and R. MacKay (eds.), *op. cit.*, p. 183.

One knowledgeable but independent enthusiast for training, Sig Prais of the National Institute of Economic and Social Research, has expressed considerable misgivings about the NCVQ philosophy on a number of grounds.[1] He points to the way in which the competence-based approach ignores developments in Europe in favour of an approach pioneered in the United States.[2] For example, despite recent emphasis on the desire to co-ordinate standards throughout the EC as part of the Single Market initiative, NVQ Level One has no counterpart elsewhere in the Community: it is too low a standard. Some Level One and even Level Two NVQs seem to require no more than a list of basic tasks which are assessed entirely in the workplace by the trainee's supervisor, and do not involve any significant written work at all.

By contrast, detailed research conducted by the National Institute in France and Germany indicates that vocational qualifications typically involve both practical and extensive written examinations, the latter emphasising general principles as well as practical applications, and entailing the need to demonstrate the ability to communicate precisely and clearly in writing about job-related matters. Successful trainees must pass both practical and written assessments.[3]

Prais also emphasises that continental examinations are externally set and externally marked. Practical tests are normally conducted in front of two or three examiners who do not know the trainee personally, under examination conditions. He expresses considerable scepticism, which it is difficult not to share, of the quality of the assessments of supervisors whose own training for this rôle is likely to be minimal, and who may be under various pressures to look favourably on trainees' performances. Although NCVQ is committed to a programme of Quality Assurance involving inspection of

[1] See, for example, S. J. Prais, 'How Europe would see the new British initiative for Standardising Vocational Qualifications', *National Institute Economic Review*, August 1989.

[2] Where, incidentally, competence-based assessment seems to have been developed as an adjunct to, rather than a substitute for, more traditional methods.

[3] In another paper, Prais has argued against the NCVQ view that written examinations of the traditional type are undesirable in principle. He points out that any assessment suffers from two sorts of errors: those associated with *validity* and *reliability*, corresponding to statistical bias and variance respectively. Although written exams suffer from the former, they are much less prone to the latter. Practical assessments of the sort advocated by NCVQ may have greater validity, but are less reliable. (See S. J. Prais, 'Vocational Qualifications in Britain and Europe: Theory and Practice', *National Institute Economic Review*, May 1991, pp. 86-92.)

assessors, this is unlikely to be exhaustive without prohibitive expense.

A final point which Prais makes is that vocational training for young people in France and Germany is seen as part of a wider educational programme, where trainees also study academic subjects beyond minimum school-leaving age. Although this has in the past also been a feature of further education in the UK, it is clear that there is little room for it in the NCVQ philosophy. As Prais puts it:

'Too much emphasis has perhaps been placed on employers' needs for personnel capable of doing their immediate jobs, and too little on the longer-term needs of the economy, and of individuals'.[1]

Education for Work?

Policy towards vocational qualifications has to be seen alongside general educational policies. The British educational system[2] has had detractors for a very long time, and they became increasingly vociferous after Prime Minister James Callaghan launched the Great Education Debate in the mid-1970s. One line of attack has concentrated on the standards achieved by average schoolchildren. Anecdotal complaints about declining standards in reading, writing and numeracy have been countered to some extent by reference to rising numbers of passes in public examinations, but less easy to dismiss has been the evidence of poor average performance by British boys and girls on standardised tests of mathematical attainment compared with their contemporaries in other countries.[3]

Another complaint relates to the disparity of resources applied and standards achieved in the British system. On the one hand, an expensive system of (largely residential) higher education, based on small institutions and what are by international standards very favourable staff-student ratios, produces a small minority of graduates—who admittedly compare favourably in

[1] S. J. Prais, 'How Europe would see the new British initiative for Standardising Vocational Qualifications', *op. cit.*, p. 53.

[2] Perhaps, more correctly, the system in England and Wales. Scotland and Northern Ireland have different and possibly more successful systems: both have much higher ratios of young people going on to higher education than is the case in England and Wales.

[3] See, for example, S. J. Prais and K. Wagner, 'Schooling standards in Britain and Germany', *National Institute Economic Review*, May 1985, and S. J. Prais, 'Educating for Productivity: Comparisons of Japanese and English Schooling and Vocational Preparation', *National Institute Economic Review*, February 1987.

many respects with their counterparts abroad.[1] On the other hand, far too many still leave school with few or no paper qualifications, and a disturbingly large minority with very low levels of literacy and numeracy.

Government activism over these matters in the last decade has been frenetic. Substantial institutional reform has occurred, with local management of schools, the removal of polytechnics and colleges from local control, and the creation of City Technology Colleges. The examination system has been changed, with the development of GCSEs, which seem likely to have increased the chances of pupils obtaining academic qualifications in future. Perhaps most importantly in the long run, the National Curriculum has been developed. This should help ensure that all pupils study a more balanced programme of subjects than has been the case in the past. The introduction of Standard Assessment Tasks should enable teachers and parents to be much clearer about children's standards and achievements at a stage when something can be done about them.

In addition to these general educational concerns, it has been increasingly argued that education in schools and colleges should bear more relation to the world of work.

There has never been a unified view of the function of education in this country. Some in the 19th century saw education as a means of social control, a perspective which goes back at least to Adam Smith[2] and arguably much further: an educated population would be less subject to wild enthusiasms and revolution. Others saw education as a strictly utilitarian task, teaching reading, writing, arithmetic and some simple technical skills appropriate to the station of life to which most people were called. For Victorian evangelicals, it was a much more high-minded operation, with its emphasis on Christianity and the classics, and with little of practical relevance other than as preparation for public administration: education for the gentleman, which some have seen as destructive of the entrepreneurial

---

[1] UK graduates are produced more quickly than their Continental counterparts. They are of a broadly uniform standard between institutions, which is clearly not the case in, say, the United States. Their courses are up-to-date and relevant (particularly in polytechnics, where content has been subject to rigorous external and internal scrutiny). Students are encouraged to be much more independent and responsible for their work than in the archaic university systems of, for example, France and Italy. The proportion of women and mature students is higher than in most other countries. UK graduates are also, with inevitable exceptions, highly employable.

[2] See J. R. Shackleton, 'Adam Smith and Education', *Higher Education Review*, Spring 1976.

spirit.[1] More recently we have seen extolled the virtues of education for citizenship, and education as a form of social engineering intended to redress class, gender and ethnic inequality.

The position of the Thatcher and Major administrations has clearly been that education in Britain requires a much more vocational slant than it has had in the past. Among the measures the Conservatives have promoted, I have already noted the advent of City Technology Colleges, originally intended as privately-funded (in practice, the overwhelming majority of funds has come from the public purse) schools in inner cities which aim at standards of excellence in work-related disciplines. Although there have been some success stories, CTCs have not taken off to the extent predicted, and the financial favouritism extended to them has made them unpopular with local authorities and existing state schools.

A greater impact has been made by the Technical and Vocational Education Initiative (TVEI). Launched in 1983, this programme now covers almost a million 14 to 18-year-olds; in 1991-92, 65 per cent of the 14-18 group are planned to be participating. TVEI aims to give students some work experience, a grasp of 'the understanding and skills which employers need',[2] and a chance to develop enterprise and initiative. In higher education, the Enterprise Initiative has been developed with rather similar aims; funds are available to develop activities promoting students' personal capabilities in a variety of ways.

Another innovation has been the development of North American-style employment 'compacts' in Urban Priority Authority areas. Here employers in the relevant area agree targets with young people in schools over such matters as higher attendance and attainments, offering in return a guarantee of a job and/or training. Compacts now cover over 92,000 young people and about 9,000 employers.

In addition, business interests are now heavily represented in the governance of schools and colleges. At least half of the members of polytechnic and college governing bodies, and a

[1] See M. J. Weiner, *English Culture and the Decline of the Industrial Spirit, 1850-1980*, Cambridge University Press, 1981.

[2] *Education and Training for the 21st Century, op. cit.*, Vol. 1, p. 9. A useful description of the workings of TVEI is given by Adam Luck, 'The TVEI Revolution', *Employment Gazette*, October 1991.

third of school governors, now represent local employers or professional bodies.[1]

Still More Vocationalism?

These developments have done much to bridge the gap which used to exist between work and school. Some argue, however, that this is not enough. They claim that the examination system (in particular GCE A-level) is too academic and dominated by the interests of the universities and, to a lesser extent, the polytechnics. The Conservatives have set their face against significant reform of A-level (though the Labour Party seeks to abolish the system in its current form). However, the Government has claimed to want to see equality between academic and vocational qualifications, with far more of the latter being offered in schools within the NVQ framework; at the moment, the Certificate of Pre-Vocational Education (available in about 60 per cent of sixth forms) is the main example. Plans have been developed for a diploma comprising A-levels, or equivalent vocational qualifications, or a combination of both.

The weaknesses of British vocational education have been a repeated theme stressed by the NIESR team, who have complained of the way in which Britain has 'persisted in keeping vocational education and training out of the education system'.[2]

So should we be going further in the direction of vocationalism in schools? Should vocational training be a key part of the National Curriculum, and should 'A'-levels be scrapped as part of this process?

Some would say not. Educational economists have frequently warned against the 'vocational school fallacy'. One of the most eminent, Professor Mark Blaug, has recently restated the argument. He claims that excessive emphasis on vocationalism 'is profoundly wrong and is actually grounded in a total misconception of what it is that makes formal education economically valuable'.[3] It assumes that schools can hope to

[1] The extent to which business 'leaders' have been asked to take on rôles of this kind has been a remarkable, though inadequately discussed, phenomenon of recent years. Whether it is greatly to the benefit of the institutions they are helping to run, or to their firms, or to neither, is a question which deserves careful study.

[2] H. Steedman, 'Improvements in Workforce Qualifications: Britain and France 1979-88', *National Institute Economic Review*, August 1990, p. 50.

[3] M. Blaug, 'The Occupational School Fallacy Once Again', Paper prepared for Universidad de Nevarra Second Economics of Education Conference: The Vocational Preparation of Young People, mimeo, pp. 1-2.

anticipate the demand for skills in the future, a pretence which the failures of 'manpower forecasting' exercises should long ago have debunked. More importantly, education's true economic significance lies in the 'hidden curriculum', described as

> 'the unintended effects of passing examinations, of spending time with classmates, of interacting with teachers, of role-play in an institution . . . in short education "socialises" students, and that is the key to the contribution of education'.[1]

As Psacharopoulos points out, these intangible consequences of education explain why,

> 'contrary to what might be expected (because of the non-specificity or non-technicality of the curriculum), social sciences, economics and law graduates are doing rather well [in many countries].'[2]

Blaug argues that heavily vocational secondary education is unpopular with students, is taught by teachers with little industrial experience or by recruits from industry who know little about teaching; equipment is frequently outdated and in any case 'the atmosphere of the classroom fails to catch the rhythm and pace' of industry. It is typically more expensive than academic schooling[3] and often offers no significant advantages in terms of job prospects.[4] Blaug quotes the American Department of Education's document *What Works*, which concludes that students with basic skills and positive work attitudes are more likely to find and keep jobs than those with vocational skills alone.[5]

[1] *Ibid.*, p. 5.

[2] G. Pscharopoulos, 'To vocationalize or not to vocationalize? That is the curriculum question', *International Review of Education*, Vol. 33, No. 2, 1987, p. 200.

[3] See Psacharopoulos, *ibid.*, p. 187.

[4] See A. L. Gustman and T. L. Steiner, 'The Relation between Vocational Training in High School and Economic Outcomes', National Bureau of Economic Research Working Paper, No. 642, 1981. They find that vocational school graduates in the United States do not have an earnings advantage over general (academic) programme high school graduates. In a wider review of the literature, J. H. Bishop, 'Occupational Training in High School: When Does it Pay Off?', *Economics of Education Review*, 1989, p. 8.11, reaches a broadly similar conclusion: vocationally-trained school students only do better when they go into a job directly related to their training—and large numbers do not do so in practice.

[5] US Department of Education, *What Works. Research about Teaching and Learning*, Washington DC, 1986.

Beware, then, of uncritical enthusiasm for further vocationalism in schools! Formal education has many rôles to play and objectives to pursue. It is attempting to prepare pupils for a variety of personal challenges in adulthood, of which those faced at work are only one, albeit important, element.

VI. THE POLITICAL ECONOMY OF TRAINING

Discussion of economic policy of all kinds has been revolutionised in recent years by the spread of interest in the economics of public choice, or the 'new political economy', associated with writers such as James Buchanan, Gordon Tullock and Anthony Downs.[1] Earlier writers on policy-making mostly discussed issues from the point of view of disinterested policy-makers who were assumed to be acting for the 'public good'—the standpoint of neo-classical welfare economics. The public choice literature (popularised by the IEA, amongst others) takes a very different stance.

The Political 'Market'

Public choice theory proceeds from the behavioural assumption that individuals will act to maximise their own utility, not only in the economic market-place but also in the political sphere. The theory posits a 'political market' in which policies are the outcome of the forces of demand and supply. On the one hand, policies are 'demanded' by groups of voters, producers and interests which will benefit from their enactment. On the other, policies are 'supplied' by politicians and bureaucrats, in exchange for votes, campaign contributions or, in the case of bureaucrats, budget appropriations.

Power in the political market-place is unevenly spread. On the demand side, the mass of consumers has little power because it is costly to organise and express their diffuse interests. The demand for policies thus tends to be concentrated among groups with specific interests in common—farmers, trade unions, professional organisations, firms in the same industry—who are individually prepared to contribute to the cost of lobbying in expectation of increased profits or other income.[2]

---

[1] Seminal works include Buchanan and Tullock's *The Calculus of Consent* (Ann Arbor: University of Michigan Press, 1962) and Downs's *An Economic Theory of Democracy* (New York: Harper and Row, 1957). A readable application of these ideas to British politics is provided by Rosalind Levacic, *Economic Policy-Making: Its Theory and Practice*, Brighton: Wheatsheaf, 1987.

[2] Generically, 'rents'. See J. M. Buchanan, R. D. Tollinson, and G. Tullock, *Toward a Theory of the Rent-seeking Society*, College Station: Texas A and M Press, 1980.

On the supply side, politicians will tend to concede those policies which appear to offer the greatest political advantage in terms of securing or retaining power. In parliamentary systems, preference is given to policies likely to catch and keep votes, particularly in marginal constituencies. The process is overlain in legislatures by 'logrolling', whereby politicians trade support for one measure in return for support for another favouring their own interests. In addition, civil servants will often have substantial power to distribute largesse in return for favours from their special-interest constituencies.

An obvious example to which this type of analysis seems to fit is the Common Agricultural Policy (CAP) of the EC, the economic disadvantages of which have been so well documented that its existence seems impossible to explain on any other grounds. Scholars and commentators have applied public choice analysis to an increasing range of policy issues, and have generally concluded that it does much to explain the pattern of government intervention in the UK and other parliamentary democracies. Official government rationale for policies is increasingly looked on with suspicion. Is such scepticism justified in relation to training?

Who Gains from Government Intervention in Training?

So far this paper has analysed the arguments for government intervention in training as if such intervention were determined purely by the objective merits of the case. But clearly this is not so. Many interest groups stand to gain from government training policy.

It is plausible that the vast expansion of publicly-funded training in the UK in the 1980s was a response to electoral considerations. Faced with rapidly accelerating unemployment, especially amongst young people, in the early 1980s, the Government had to be seen to be doing something.[1] Whereas earlier governments might have chosen to boost aggregate demand or subsidise bankrupt firms, such possibilities were closed off by the Thatcher administration's other policy commitments. The 'training' label can be seen as initially something of a rationalisation of programmes which, as has been seen, had at the beginning little skill-enhancement content and were used to disguise the real extent of unemployment.

The Labour Party's recent enthusiasm for training is also

[1] Particularly in view of the inner-city riots which accompanied rising unemployment.

[77]

explicable in these terms. The Party has of course always been suspicious of the virtues of the market, but one by one many of its interventionist options were foreclosed as a result of economic change or the failure of previous experiments. With national-isation, active demand management, planning, exchange rate manipulation and import controls now apparently permanently off the agenda, a training 'revolution' appears the one remaining way of influencing the development of the economy. The unions' traditional support is another factor. With Labour's reluctance to repeal the industrial relations legislation of the last decade, emphasis on training is a 'sweetener' to organised labour which is also acceptable to a wider public.

Unions, in Britain as elsewhere, are strongly in favour of increased formal training provision. Their motives vary, but we have already noted the way in which qualifications can be used as a means of reducing competition in the labour market. Historically, British unions have defended trained (skilled) labour against 'dilution' by the unskilled; their co-operation in relaxing the rules during two World Wars was predicated on normal service being resumed as soon as possible after the cessation of hostilities. Wherever possible, they tend to press for higher entry qualifications to jobs, a policy which enhances 'rents' to existing workers.

Employers, too, hope to gain from government intervention in training. As suggested earlier, public funding often takes the place of training which firms would otherwise finance them-selves. In the past, too, employers who provide training have often supported industry levies in order to equalise the burden of training costs which other firms had previously avoided.

Then there is the growing army of 'trainers'—a term which embraces private and public sector organisations and individuals which draw their incomes from providing training. In a period when higher education has been squeezed—at least by com-parison with what universities and polytechnics had come to expect—training has been an area where funds have been available in some abundance. Unsurprisingly, many erstwhile educators have become born-again trainers, pushing for an expansion of publicly-funded training.[1]

One suspects, too, that this may not only be true of academics

---

[1] In rather the same way as E. G. West tells us that teachers and school inspectors promoted compulsory education in the last century (see earlier reference in Section III, p. 28, fn. 2).

in their teaching rôles. The bulk of significant published research on training in this country has been funded, directly or indirectly, by the Department of Employment or the Training Agency and its predecessors. Most of this work has tended to take for granted a belief that market failures are common in training, without seriously examining some of the counter-indications discussed in this *Hobart Paper*.

Furthermore, we have already seen evidence of classic interest-group activity in the new TECs. First set up as a more efficient means of delivering training policies determined by central government, they are now establishing themselves as a strong political interest in their own right, calling for increased government spending in a way which goes far beyond what civil servants would have been permitted to do when they were running training schemes.

Mixed Motives

Of course the interests outlined here are only part of the picture. Critics of the public choice approach have rightly pointed out that politicians and interest groups are not all as venal as might be inferred from the previous paragraphs. The individuals involved may very well be convinced that the policies they advocate are good for the nation as well as themselves. In some instances they may be correct. But in any case real people are not simply narrowly economic in motivation; their motives are mixed and often confused. Those who work in training have a natural tendency to want to promote their field of interest and secure the support and appreciation of their peers. Given their specialist knowledge and concern, trainers find it hard not to be impatient with politicians and to assume that specialists have a better understanding of the public interest.

Nevertheless, any evaluation of training policy would be incomplete without an awareness that, here as in any other area of policy, there is a generous element of special pleading involved. Policies which give interest groups greater power and influence should always be examined with considerable scepticism.

VII. SUMMING UP

This paper has examined the propositions that the UK has a seriously underskilled work-force and that a massively increased investment in training is a necessary condition for the country's economic regeneration and advance.

Despite the widespread popularity of these beliefs, the paper has cast doubt on them from the viewpoint of a sceptical economist. We have seen that there is little evidence to support the view that the total quantity of training is closely correlated to a country's economic performance and that there is no necessary connection between stocks of skilled labour and productivity.

While there may be the possibility of market failure in the area of 'general' training, there is in practice a high level of private provision of such training, and this provision seems to respond rationally to market signals.

Indeed, we have seen that there is very considerable explicit and implicit expenditure on all forms of training in this country. On some definitions it may be costing us more than 10 per cent of GDP each year. Some other countries may spend rather more, but this is not necessarily beneficial. It is possible that labour markets distorted by government intervention may even be spending *too much* on training, particularly as some types of training may do little to enhance productivity and serve rather different functions.

International comparisons of training and education do not always support the view that the UK system is uniquely inadequate. Institutional set-ups and practices differ considerably, but in some areas—for example, higher education and the provision of genuine work experience for young trainees—the UK may have lessons to offer as well as to learn.

However, an examination of recent training policy in the UK suggests that there are question-marks against some current and planned initiatives, and that economic analysis could usefully have a larger rôle to play. This is especially true in view of the array of vested interests lined up in support of the expansion of training.

None of this should be taken—though it probably will be—as

[80]

hostility towards training as such. In a complex and rapidly changing economy, a high level of training and education will always be necessary. However, hesitation is an appropriate response when we are asked to spend increasing amounts of public money on policies of doubtful merit, or to impose obligations on employers or individuals to meet their skills requirements in a particular way, or to force education into a vocational straitjacket.

In the 1980s we learnt to be much less trusting of claims that governments could outguess the market over a wide range of economic activities. And given the endless claims on the public purse, even those wishing to see some expansion of public spending in other areas ought to be less trusting of those who believe they know which skills will benefit the economy better than the individuals and firms involved. The ability to use informed scepticism against plausible-sounding remedies for economic ailments is a skill which, unfortunately, no amount of training is likely to impart.

GLOSSARY

Age-Earnings Profile: Relationship (usually illustrated diagrammatically) between age and earnings for representative individuals as they move through time.

Aggregate Production Function: Mathematical expression linking an economy's total output to measures of the inputs of the services of the factors of production such as land, labour and capital. Various functions have been used in empirical work; the most popular have been the Cobb-Douglas and the Constant Elasticity of Substitution (CES) functions.

Deadweight Loss: In the context of training, that part of the increase in training as a result of a government scheme which simply replaces trainees that firms would otherwise take on. In welfare economics this term has another, though related, meaning.

Discounted Present Value: The value of future payments or receipts in terms of what they are worth today. This reflects the fact that resources tied up in a project have an opportunity cost— the rate of return available elsewhere, generically known as the *discount rate*. The present value of a sum of money to be received in the future thus falls as the discount rate rises.

Displacement Effect: Reduction in employment or training opportunities for one group as a result of increasing them for another group.

Economies of Scale: Reduction in the long-run average costs of production as the size of plant increases. There are various reasons for this; one is the geometrical truism that doubling linear dimensions more than doubles volume.

Elasticity of Substitution: Measure of the responsiveness of the ratio in which productive factors are employed to changes in the relative prices of their services.

External Benefits: Benefits from an economic activity which flow to those who are not directly involved in the activity as buyer or seller.

General Training: Training which enhances the value of an individual's skills to a range of potential employers.

Government Failure: Government's inability to carry out efficiently some task, or to benefit voters in the way it intended.

Internal Labour Market: Firm or organisation within which workers compete for pay and promotion, but from which 'outsiders' are excluded and thus do not directly compete with existing workers. Typically, recruitment is limited to only one or two *ports of entry*. ILMs, because of the privileged conditions available to 'insiders', may have an excess of applicants to jobs at these ports of entry.

Market Failure: Situation where the free market produces an economically inefficient outcome.

Multiple Regression: Statistical method of determining the influence of a range of variables on a variable in which we are interested. In principle, the separate effects of the *explanatory variables* can be estimated. In practice, there are often considerable difficulties in doing this as a result of such problems as *multi-collinearity*, where the explanatory variables are not independent of each other.

Opportunity Cost: Cost of an activity in terms of the best alternative use to which resources could otherwise be put.

Private Rate of Return: The (internal) rate of return to an investment is that discount rate which just equates the discounted present value of the costs to that of the returns. In the case of the PRR, economists are concerned only with the costs incurred by, and the benefits accruing to, the relevant individual or firm.

Risk Aversity: Unwillingness to accept a 'fair' gamble; desire to protect oneself from the consequences of risk. Thus a risk-averse individual will insure against a loss, even though the *expected value* of the loss (what you could expect to lose on average over repeated trials) is less than the cost of the insurance premium.

Social Rate of Return: In calculating the SRR we allow for benefits which accrue to, and costs which are incurred by, members of society other than those directly involved in the investment decision. (*See* **Private Rate of Return.**)

Specific Training: Training which enhances skills in a way which is valuable only to one employer.

Substitution Effect: In the training context, the substitution of government-funded trainees for other groups of (more expensive) workers by firms aiming to reduce costs.

Value Marginal Productivity: The addition to the total value of output produced as a result of employing one extra unit of a factor of production (usually labour).

QUESTIONS FOR DISCUSSION

1. What are the potential sources of 'market failure' in the provision of training?

2. What are the potential 'government failures' in training?

3. What factors determine (a) the private rate of return on training, and (b) the social rate of return?

4. Why does the extent of training provision differ between firms?

5. Why do you think that few firms claim to evaluate the benefits from training? Does this mean that economic analysis of the costs and benefits is irrelevant?

6. What are the strengths and weaknesses of the German 'dual' system of vocational training?

7. Why do large numbers of employees work in jobs for which they are over-qualified?

8. How do 'displacement effects' reduce the attractiveness of government training schemes?

9. Does Britain require a standardised framework for vocational qualifications?

10. Why have pressures for more government spending on, and promotion of, training increased in the last decade?

FURTHER READING

Barnett, C., *The Audit of War*, London: Macmillan, 1986.

Becker, G. S., *Human Capital*, New York: National Bureau of Economic Research, 2nd edition, 1975.

Dept. of Employment, *Education and Training for the 21st Century* Cm. 1536, London: HMSO, 1991.

Dept. of Employment, *Training in Britain: A Study of Funding, Activity and Attitudes,* Vol. 1: *Employers' Activities*; Vol. 2: *Market Perspectives*; Vol. 3: *Employers' Perspectives on Human Resouces*; Vol. 4: *Individual Perspectives*, London: HMSO, 1989.

Metcalf, D., *The Economics of Vocational Training: Past Evidence and Future Considerations*, World Bank Staff Working Paper No. 713, Washington DC, 1985.

Sheldrake, J., and S. Vickerstaff, *The History of Industrial Training in Britain*, Aldershot: Avebury, 1987.

Stevens, J., and R. MacKay (eds.), *Training and Competitiveness*, London: National Economic Development Office/Kogan Page, 1991.

West, E. G., *Education and the Industrial Revolution*, London: Batsford, 1975.

The National Institute of Economic and Social Research has published a large number of detailed studies of aspects of training, mainly in the *National Institute Economic Review*. Fifteen of these studies are gathered together with an introduction by S. J. Prais in *Productivity, Education and Training: Britain and Other Countries Compared*, London: NIESR, 1990.

Beyond Universities:
A New Republic of the Intellect
SIR DOUGLAS HAGUE, CBE

Summary

Universities in the UK have traditionally operated under a common system which institutionalises important restrictive practices. They have operated in a cartel whose output has been regulated by government. The individual firms (i.e. universities) are allocated quotas of students by government, and fees and salaries are set in ways that are typical of a classic cartel. The university cartel is underpinned by a further monopoly, granted as of right to each university. In the UK nobody can award degrees unless empowered to do so by royal charter or by the Secretary of State for Education and Science.

Professor Sir Douglas Hague takes this argument a stage further by stating that the current stage of economic development is strongly based on the acquisition, analysis and transmission of information and on its application. Universities will therefore be forced to share, or even give up, part of their role as repositories of information and as power bases for ideas transmitted through teaching and writing.

In this richly original *Hobart Paper*, Professor Sir Douglas Hague identifies the challenges which universities will have to meet and argues that, if these can be overcome, universities should be able to survive both as competitors and complements of the knowledge industries over the coming decades.

The Author

Professor Sir Douglas Hague, CBE, is Honorary Visiting Professor at Manchester Business School, where he was previously Professor of Managerial Economics and Deputy Director. He is author of numerous works on economics and management, and was Chairman of the Economic and Social Research Council, 1983-87. (A full note on the author can be found on page 8.)

ISBN 0-255 36244-7   Hobart Paper 115

The Institute of Economic Affairs
2 Lord North Street, Westminster
London SW1P 3LB

£6.95   Telephone: 071-799 3745

Published in 1992

OVERSEAS INVESTMENTS, CAPITAL GAINS AND THE BALANCE OF PAYMENTS

CLIFF PRATTEN

Since 1945, the United Kingdom's share of world manufacturing output has declined from an artificially high 25 per cent of world trade and had stabilised at just below 10 per cent by the late 1980s. The nature of exports has also changed, reflecting the decline in traditional industries such as steel and shipbuilding and the emergence of the knowledge-based industries such as financial services and electronics.

In this *Research Monograph* the balance of payments of the United Kingdom is thoroughly examined; the contribution of services such as banking, insurance and shipping has ensured that the balance of payments is in much better shape than is generally contended.

For example, capital gains on overseas investment since 1979, made possible by the abolition of exchange control, have made a contribution of more than four times the current account deficit over the corresponding period.

As recent international events have shown, the concept of the nation state is still alive. The ability to measure the effects of both outward and inward investment across national boundaries will be fundamental to understanding the economic strengths of each nation.

ISBN 0-255 36303-6   Research Monograph 48   **£7·95**

THE INSTITUTE OF ECONOMIC AFFAIRS
2 Lord North Street, Westminster
London SW1P 3LB   Telephone: 071-799 3745